Leading in the Belly of the Beast

Leading in the Belly of the Beast

School Leadership in a System Designed to Fail

Edited by
Trevor Gardner

ROWMAN & LITTLEFIELD
Lanham • Boulder • New York • London

Published by Rowman & Littlefield
A wholly owned subsidary of The Rowman & Littlefield Publishing Group, Inc.
4501 Forbes Boulevard, Suite 200, Lanham, Maryland 20706
www.rowman.com

6 Tinworth Street, London SE11 5AL, United Kingdom

British Library Cataloguing in Publication Information Available

Library of Congress Cataloging-in-Publication Data

Library of Congress Control Number: 2020940704

ISBN: 978-1-4758-5210-3 (cloth : alk. paper)
ISBN: 978-1-4758-5211-0 (pbk. : alk. paper)
ISBN: 978-1-4758-5212-7 (electronic)

♾️™ The paper used in this publication meets the minimum requirements of American National Standard for Information Sciences—Permanence of Paper for Printed Library Materials, ANSI/NISO Z39.48-1992.

This book is dedicated to the tens of millions of brilliant young stars in our nation who do all they can to survive and thrive in schools every day—and to the educators who give everything they have to create spaces of excitement, joy, empowerment, and liberation.

You must understand that in the attempt to correct so many generations of bad faith and cruelty, when it is operating not only in the classroom but in society, you will meet the most fantastic, the most brutal, and the most determined resistance. There is no point in pretending this won't happen.

—James Baldwin, 1963

Contents

Preface

On the Importance of Diverse Voices

Trevor Gardner

When I first envisioned this book, I heard different voices, all brilliant but separate from one another, sharing their insights about leading within an institution that was set up to fail. It would be grounded in theory, yet practical, something new and experienced school leaders alike could pick up and explore for insights to utilize immediately. My intention was to gather the voices of leaders who had weathered storms in the belly of the beast, had persisted, and were continuing to find ways to successfully transform their schools and institutions.

What I came to realize as we embarked on this nearly two-year project, through multiple writing retreats, innumerable conversations, and continuous feedback, and revision cycles, is that the diversity of voices and experiences the authors bring, diversity both in terms of our identities as well as the contexts in which we teach and lead, made the book both a journey and a destination. This diversity is the power and potential of all work we do in education. We are stronger, smarter, and more courageous together than we ever will be working individually.

So, who are we and what are our educational contexts?

Milton is an African American man who grew up in the suburbs of the Bay Area and dropped out of high school before going on to become a middle school teacher for many years. He continues to lead for educational transformation in multiple contexts, inside and outside of schools.

Meredith is a white, Jewish American woman who began her career teaching in New York City public schools before moving to New Haven where she founded a small interdistrict magnet school.

Eran is a Sri Lankan American woman whose experience as one of only a few students of color in her high school led her to become a teacher and leader at a Catholic all-girls high school. She has also worked in cross-school collaboration with a wide range of schools—public, private, and charter—to develop student leadership, professional development, and curricular programs for over six years.

Timothy is a white American man who grew up in Seattle before moving to the Bay Area. He began as a youth development worker in his early twenties before moving into the high school classroom. He has spent his career teaching at public district schools in San Francisco and Oakland and leading pathway and school design work.

Kristin is a Mexican American woman who was born and raised in Los Angeles. She taught English in two of the largest public high schools in Los Angeles from 1987 to 2006 before becoming a school leader at a charter school in South Los Angeles.

Trevor is a white American man who grew up in Northern California. He has taught and led at district schools in both SFUSD and OUSD as well as three different public charter schools.

There is no single way to lead in the belly of the beast and no formulaic profile of a transformative school leader. There are no silver bullets or simple answers. Each of us has stumbled, struggled, and grown into the leader we are through peregrination and conversation with the myriad young people, families, communities, and fellow educators we have served (their voices are heard through the pages of this book), whose identities represent the diversity of the society we inhabit.

But not diversity in the superficial, easy celebration that avoids conflict and remains aloof from the ways that our differences have been used throughout history to divide, conquer, enslave, and oppress. Not the diversity that invites you to the table only to ignore your input and get back to business as usual. Not the diversity that needs to be *managed* so we can maintain the status quo.

Rather, we need to leverage our diversity as an asset and do the hard and painful, but ultimately liberating, work of engaging deeply with ourselves and each other, with the fullness and complexity of all who are a part of the conversation.

Leveraging our diversity is our way forward; it is the way to defeat the beast.

Below, each author weighs in on the power of this diversity in writing this book and in their work in education.

Eran DeSilva: There is no singular experience of being American. To truly understand our diverse local and global community, we need to invite everyone to the table and encourage them to share their stories and use their voices. I feel like educators sometimes work in isolation or in silos. We sometimes get caught up thinking that our school site or our students are different from others. But as I heard the stories and struggles and insights of my colleagues from a variety of schools, I saw the common threads of yearning for justice, a commitment to justice, and fierce love for their students. We built solidarity and we drew strength and hope from one another to persevere even when we were frustrated by the slow steps to change.

Kristin Botello: One thing I have learned about myself in all my years educating young people is that I can only clarify my thinking and my mission through constant reflection and revision that results from interacting with my peers, some with whom I disagree and some who validate and confirm my commitments. As servant leaders, we need each other. We need those who inspire *us*, model for *us*, push *us*, and give *us* hope. And real hope comes from those who, as my friend, Tim describes, are committed to doing "the work."

As a school leader working in my own context of working class Los Angeles, I assumed that every school leader had the same struggles. Obviously, poor kids in LA are the same as poor kids in Connecticut or the Bay, right? Wrong! I learned how many stories are similar and yet how many stories represent vastly different realities—and these are all young inner-city folks. This isn't even incorporating the young minds and lives in private schools, where some of my counterparts work. Working with these amazing educators has taught me to continue to look in the mirror and not just out the window, because an educator who is striving to create justice and equity is open to diverse voices and experiences.

Meredith Gavrin: For me, as a white woman teaching primarily students of color for more than twenty years, working with a diverse staff at my own school and learning from an incredible, diverse group of educators through organizations I've worked with has been critical to my own learning and my ability to serve my students fully. And preparing our students to live, work, love, and thrive in a diverse world requires a multiplicity of perspectives and voices. There is no other way.

Milton Reynolds: Engaging with diversity is essential to achieving. Our different lived experiences and knowledge must be engaged to help students develop the cognitive scaffolds that are able to hold complexity and nurture critical thought. The power of these collective assets was quite evident in the process of writing this book. The process demonstrated what is always true, we are smarter as a collective than we are individually.

Our different lived realities, experiences of navigating identification, engaging with scholarship, and working in different contexts helped to create a rich tapestry of wisdom that amplified and enhanced what each of us contributed individually.

Timothy Bremner: I believe deeply in the need and power of collective attitudes and beliefs to drive collaborative action. The intersectionality of identities, multiple perspectives, and varied voices is necessary to work together to transform oppressive systems toward a healthy and sustainable future. Each person in this anthology really brings a different personal experience and a different professional experience. Each leader works to transform the beast in a different context; however, we are united by common critique of oppressive systems of education that are designed to fail students of color. This shows our challenge and therefore charge, which is to work toward justice that goes beyond public, charter, and private schools and even schools themselves. It is a way of finding co-conspirators, being in relation, and working together to do co-create our present and our future.

Trevor Gardner: This book would not have been conceived without the diversity of voices on display throughout the chapters. I have been in conversation with the other authors in *Leading in the Belly of the Beast* for many years, some for my entire career in education. My thoughts and actions as an educator and a leader are a direct result of the ways they—and myriad other students, teachers, families, and community members—have inspired, pushed, challenged, and supported me in my journey.

The process of writing this book has replicated that journey for all of us, perhaps in different ways, but each author has transformed and grown through their engagement with this project. My hope for the reader is that you will be open in a similar way to the voices that will speak to you through these chapters. They may not all resonate in the same way; they may not all feel perfectly relevant to your context; they may well challenge and confront you in ways you did not prepare for, but they all come from a unique and authentic place of lived experience that has much to offer.

While writing this book, we learned that we shared many common beliefs, influences, and practices as leaders but that we also had incredibly divergent backgrounds and leadership styles. Each author in this book has found ways to be highly effective but each way is different. Diversity lesson #1: there is no single right way to lead.

During the process of crafting, writing, revising, and discussing, we noticed some things about our group dynamics—for example, patriarchy was showing up in our conversations in the amount of air time we were taking up. We were forced to pause, discuss this dynamic directly, and address it honestly. We engaged with various challenges related to our identities and perspectives during our time together and each time we did our best to confront them.

To ignore the beast rearing its head in the midst of our writing retreats would be to ignore the very purpose for which we were writing. Diversity lesson #2: true diversity is not always easy or nice; we need to build trust and be willing to challenge and push one another.

Each author came to the table with a general idea of what our chapters would focus on. However, most of us did not begin this journal with a fully fleshed out vision. It was through our Socratic discussions, our sharing of ideas, and our offering of different perspectives and experiences that *Leading in the Belly of the Beast* really came to fruition. Diversity lesson #3: we are always stronger and better working together than working in isolation.

Acknowledgments

Eran DeSilva: I would like to thank and give much love to my children who humble me and teach me every day to be my best self. To all of my students over the last twenty years, you inspire me to commit every day to learn more and make our world a more just, compassionate place. Special thanks to the women who have helped me find my voice and encouraged me to use my voice this year: Megan, Tanisha, and Wendy.

Kristin Botello: I would like to dedicate my work to my parents, Mike and Josie Botello, and my eight siblings, who made me the woman and educator that I am. I am nothing without my partner in life, Michael, or my children, who give me purpose and inspire me daily. Finally, I dedicate my writing to those students and teachers at Animo Jackie Robinson, whose stories I tell and whose *animo* truly pushes me to be brave, to be better, and to continue to discover myself and my potential as a human being through the work that I do.

Meredith Gavrin: I would like to acknowledge that without Greg Baldwin, who started out as the teacher in the classroom next door and became my husband and school co-founder, none of my adventures in education would have taken place. And to Elijah, Caleb, and Mia—thank you for teaching me something every day. I love you all.

Milton Reynolds: A special note of appreciation is due to my lovely wife Danae Reynolds, an amazing educator in her own right, for her thoughtful and candid suggestions. To Rick Ayers, much love for your encouragement, the sharing of your writing craft, and for practicing daily what you preach.

Timothy Bremner: I would like to acknowledge and thank my family, friends, colleagues, and thinkers who have both provided the love and support to become who I am, and opportunities to see how my own privileges and those like me must be interrogated and utilized for the pursuit of a just society. Frankie, Sydney, and Elliott: I love you.

Trevor Gardner: I want to humbly acknowledge and appreciate all of the students, families, fellow educators, and community members who have taught me everything I know about being a teacher and leader. I recognize that I stand upon your shoulders. Equally as important, I give thanks to my mom and dad and my family who have supported me unconditionally throughout my career; to Shikira, with whom I walk hand in hand on this life journey; and to Omari, who is my greatest teacher and most profound inspiration.

Finally, special gratitude to my fellow authors on this book for trusting, believing, and taking the journey with me—and to Tony Lepire and Rick Ayers, two of my most influential writing mentors.

Introduction

Naming the Beast

Leading in the Belly of the Beast is the first of two books of essays from school leaders who are navigating paths toward transformative results within a school system that is not set up for the success of all students in this country, especially Black, Indigenous, and People of Color (BIPOC)[1] students and those living in poverty. They begin from the premise that the system of education in the United States, since its inception, has functioned to maintain the racial, cultural, and economic status quo—and to maintain divisions among these racial, cultural, and class groups.

This may appear to be a far-flung assertion to some, but to those working intimately with the education system, especially those serving our most marginalized and underserved students, the evidence, as you will read throughout these pages, is unavoidable.

There are several excellent texts out there on social justice leadership and leadership for equity that provide important insights, strategies, and solutions. However, this book is unique because its authors begin from seeing the system not as broken, but rather as functioning to attain many of the outcomes it has, throughout its history, intended to achieve.

From Thomas Jefferson's contention that schools should serve to find the "best geniuses [to] be raked from the rubbish annually" (1782), to the eugenics-rooted IQ testing of the early 1900s, through the racist outcomes in school discipline practices today, the education system has always privileged some and subjugated others. Consequently, educators and leaders working alongside their students toward their liberation and transformation must "go for broke" in the words of James Baldwin's 1963 speech to teachers (1998) by confronting, dismantling, and rebuilding the system from within.

It is important that we step back for a moment and discuss what we mean by "the beast" in the context of schooling. It is a fraught allusion but one

1

that feels accurate and truthful, even as its pervasiveness makes it difficult to define with precision. The beast functions both externally in the form of overlapping systems of oppression that shape and alter the lives of students and communities, and internally as the impact of these systems plays out on various levels and in multiple spaces within schools.

The beast wears many faces. It manifests itself in systems, structures, and policies (i.e., immigration policies that keeps millions of families living in perpetual fear or racist discipline systems that produce inequitable outcomes). It plays out financially in the extreme under-resourcing of public education in general and the disparity in funding and resources between the privileged and the disregarded (an Oakland teacher could commute just thirty miles and increase their salary by over $30,000 with the same level of experience). It expresses itself through the attitudes, beliefs, and values, both intentional and unintentional, of those working in various institutions with which students interact every day. And it asserts itself in the overwhelming conditions that lead to a majority of educators leaving their positions within five years of beginning their teaching careers.

Ultimately, for schools to equitably and justly serve all young people in this country to realize their full human potential, we will need the imagination, the courage, the organization, and the collective energy to dismantle and rebuild the entire system of education as it exists today. This is the dream. We must work for such radical change—but while we are working toward that dream, we have tens of millions of young people showing up in our classrooms every day ready to learn.

Every author in *Leading in the Belly of the Beast* has made an intentional choice to remain in schools, even after many years of working inside the ugly viscera and witnessing its potential for destruction. We have chosen to stay because we have also experienced the profound possibility for transformation, liberation, and triumph even within the belly of the beast.

This book is written by and for school leaders. It aspires to capture the experiences of these leaders in a way that balances the practical and the theoretical, through both a narrative and an analytical approach, so that readers can see their schools and their students within these pages and take with them insights, practices, and tools to help them better lead their own communities. Additionally, and equally as important, each author infuses their chapter with personal narratives about how their experiences and identities have contributed to the leaders they have become.

In chapter 1, Milton Reynolds offers a historical, political, and social framework to more deeply understand the context in which schools operate today.

In chapter 2, Trevor Gardner discusses significant challenges he has faced with staff at his school and how he roots himself in a set of Core Values to continue to build a culture of community, solidarity, and purpose.

In chapter 3, Kristin Botello introduces her concept of "tenacious love" and how she marshals it to serve her students and maintain a school that feels like an "oasis" in a neighborhood that is often neglected and forgotten.

In chapter 4 Meredith Gavrin advocates for treating teachers as the true professionals they are and explains a key component of her leadership, which involves protecting the space for teachers to think critically, be creative, and take risks in creating genuinely engaging learning spaces for their students.

In chapter 5, Eran DeSilva places student voice front and center and explores how, as a leader, she facilitates various ways in which students lead the way for her staff and her school.

Finally, in chapter 6, Timothy Bremner discusses the critical importance of collaboration and collectivism in building a school culture that sustains and persists even in the midst of incredibly challenging work.

NOTE

1. The acronym BIPOC refers to Black, Indigenous, and People of Color. The authors choose to use the term BIPOC over the common term "people of color" throughout the text to acknowledge the unique experiences of black and Indigenous people in the United States as a result of the history of racialized slavery and indigenous genocide. While there are many common experiences shared by all people of color in this society due to their experiences of being nonwhite in a culture where whiteness dominates, there are critical ways that black and Indigenous people's experiences are unique and must be identified as such. Of course, it is important to acknowledge that all people of color in the United States have a unique set of experiences, so any term seeking to label all nonwhite groups together is inherently limited. The authors use the term BIPOC in order to try to balance the particular and the collective.

Chapter 1

The Dangers of Definition

Milton Reynolds

Colorblind talk furthers racial power not through the direct articulation of racial differences but rather by obscuring the operation of racial power, protecting it from challenge, and permitting ongoing racialization through racially coded methods.

—Claire Jean Kim

INTRODUCTION

Were any of us to never step foot in a classroom we would still develop significant knowledge about the world. In the case of specific interests, this knowledge would be encyclopedic. All human beings have the capacity to learn. If we truly believe this, then how do we explain the enduring continuity in the patterns of disparate outcomes among particular student populations?

Understanding these patterns and effectively interrupting the predictability of these outcomes can only come from a deeper historical reckoning with the systems we inhabit. This engagement with the past is necessary to situate ourselves within the longer story of education such that we can understand our positionality within it, what that reveals, and also what it obfuscates.

Among the questions we must reckon with as educators are to what extent the experience of schooling interferes with a natural process and how we begin to understand the all-too-predictable patterns of racialized outcomes in order to interrupt them?

Being an effective and transformative practitioner in the belly of the beast requires a deeper reckoning with the understanding that *we, as educators, are functionaries of the beast.* We cannot effectively meet the needs of all students, especially those most vulnerable, without acknowledging this fundamental reality.

Our educational system is not broken. In fact, from a historical perspective, schools do exactly what they were designed to do. They identify, measure, separate, and sort along predictable lines, producing outcomes that are entirely consistent with the ideological drivers that informed the development of the systems we inhabit. Schools do so however at a tremendous cost. This human toll is borne by the collective, but the consequences accrue asymmetrically and tragically.

As a career educator, one who has worked in several schools, has helped to create two others, and served as an outside service provider to dozens more, Milton Reynolds finds this basic level of understanding to be elusive, rarely present in the discourse informing daily practice at schools. Historical contextualization is often absent in discussions of school reform. In the absence of such understanding, students, educators, schools, communities, and ultimately our entire society is done irreparable harm. This absence of reckoning also costs us time, resources, good intentions, and human capital we cannot afford to lose.

The failure to challenge centuries of institutional commitment to racial subordination, domination, exploitation, and segregation causes us to continue patterns of human wastage and divestment that have served to exacerbate preexisting inequality. Our unwillingness to acknowledge the intentionality of these investments, their foundational nature, and myriad legacies encourages patterns of destructive mythology that limits our ability to make democracy inclusive, to close the gap between the articulated credo and our lived realities.

As our demographic transformation propels us toward a moment in which Black, Indigenous, and People of Color (BIPOC), and other minoritized communities will soon constitute the majority population in the United States, our willingness to countenance the consistent racialized outcomes of our educational system represents a national crisis. We can no longer afford to neglect our past and pretend we can build a collective future; we will have to face the past with honesty, clarity, and courage to awaken a new chapter in American democracy.

School is the place where this work must happen, as our schools are among the primary institutions from whence these false narratives of biological essentialism that fuel these patterns are initiated and nurtured. The belief that these racialized outcomes are rooted in biology, cultural, and increasingly genetic differences rather than the policies and practices that systematically invest in some while simultaneously divesting others categorically, is a deeply held, though dangerously distorting fantasy.

However, we need not stay stuck; we can shift these understandings. Schools also hold the greatest potential to support future generations in redefining the rules of the game, reimagining how our society might actually function in a just and inclusive fashion. The current patterns of inequitable outcomes are not inevitable, we must believe that.

By situating our craft as a direct response to past and present deleterious processes, practices, structures, and belief systems we can more effectively serve all our students and the larger society. Through such shifts we can equip students with the knowledge, skills, and opportunities necessary to *become agents of their own transformation and liberation.*

THE DILEMMA OF FRAMING
LEARNING AS PERFORMANCE

The act of doing without deeper reflection on the purpose or objectives of action seems to be rooted in the learned behavior of schooling itself. In many respects, the experience of learning has become a kind of performance; one could say a performance of "fitness" if we want to speak candidly and historically. In classrooms around the nation, students are asked to engage with content, often curated primarily by their teachers in order to demonstrate their understanding in exchange for the affirmation and recognition of said teacher.

The cultivation of this short-term engagement/reward relationship with learning may diminish the value of those investments or divorce them from the long-term, context-specific application of that knowledge. Learning is a process rather than an event, though critical observation of the vast majority of classrooms would suggest otherwise.

Classrooms that encourage students to simply provide answers rather than generate questions about the world around them and their place within it, tend to foster a performative relationship with learning. By focusing on demonstrations of knowing rather than application of that knowledge, we do students and society a profound disservice.

Curiosity is the gateway to learning. Critical thinking comes from being willing to question and becoming comfortable with the dissonance these questions often generate. Encouraging students to expand their frontiers of knowledge and redefining the boundaries of their understanding is a process that requires patience, the willingness to embrace tension, uncertainty, and most certainly, requires educators who embolden their students to question. Educators who demonstrate an ability to predictably create such learning spaces tend to exemplify these traits themselves.

Many students engage in this process of performative learning with little to no conflict, as they see no gaps between the curated content and their own lives. This way of learning "to get to the next step" is frankly consistent with the ways most of us have been socialized to view education as a meritocratic system of advancement. Some students, often the more privileged ones who have mastered the art of endurance and pretending interest, may also be sensitive to curricular disconnects and contradictions, but have been conditioned to be nice, not speak up.

They have become all too aware that compliance and acceptance are more frequently rewarded classroom behaviors. However, for students whose life experiences generate different or contradictory understandings of the world, these acts of performance can become an existential threat.

The decision to perform knowing, particularly in relationship to a curricular journey in which one's lived experience is rarely evident, can negate or diminish one's sense of self, the value of one's community, culture, or ways of knowing and inhabiting the world. By divorcing learning from relevance and ultimately application, we create unnecessary impediments to engagement.

Teachers' desire to create calm, comfortable, and predictable learning environments often comes at a cost to students. Recognizing the teacher is the primary arbiter of norms in classrooms, we have to ask, whose norms of comfort or safety, a word increasingly in use, define what is acceptable, legitimate, and at what cost? Rooted in assumptions of universality, the imposition of a particular set of norms limits the expression of different lived experiences and the intellectual assets associated with them.

Too often, those who choose not to embrace these norms are pushed further to the margins of the classroom. In this regard, the demographic mismatch between the current teaching force and student population represents a significant structural challenge. In 2014–2015 the percentage of students of color within the student population of the United States was 50.3 percent. By 2045, the majority population of the nation will be BIPOC. Our teaching force doesn't mirror these trends, nor is it likely to any time in the near future. Currently, our teaching force is roughly 80 percent white, representationally speaking, way out of skew (Fay 2018).

Prior to school desegregation efforts, classroom dynamics differed. Patterns of segregation also generated economic and civic opportunities for educators and administrators of color. Reflecting on his father's recounting of attending segregated schools as a child, it is difficult for Reynolds not to speculate how schools might function differently had equality of funding been pursued rather than desegregation.

Reynolds didn't romanticize the differential access to resources or other dehumanizing aspects of segregation in the south, but he has often, spoken fondly of his African American teachers, the care they showed for him, the power of their practice, and the sense of collective endeavor and community uplift he shared with his fellow students. His narrative was always starkly contrasted with the presentation of desegregation most experienced in schools, of desegregation as a redemptive and overwhelmingly positive experience for African Americans.

Needless to say, those master narratives, more often than not, are devoid of the history of segregation impacting Latinx, Asian, Indigenous, and African American students in California. Segregation was presented as a quirk of the past, something innately southern, never to touch other parts of our nation. Having access to those broader histories would be useful, not only for what they illuminate, but also for the important questions such exposure is likely to generate. To be fair, teachers would themselves have to know this history to teach it. Unfortunately, deeper national commitments to colorblind discourse continue to function as an impediment to acquiring this essential knowledge.

This is not to suggest that white identifying educators can't teach or play a meaningful role in the lives of students of color. Not only would that dismiss the powerful educators who invest in and effectively cultivate the talents of children of color and other marginalized students every day, but also my professional experience. Having witnessed a number of educators whose skill, craft, dedication to their students and positive student outcomes defy the patterns, we know this is not true.

Essentializing the limitations of white teachers in this sense is no more useful than essentializing the "failures" of marginalized students. However, it is imperative that we grapple with the differential experiences of socialization in a society founded on the normalization of human hierarchies, in which whiteness is positioned as the normative standard against which other groups are measured.

In order to address these dynamics, we will have to engage with the history of how difference has been defined and the role schools play in that process. This has proven to be a difficult turnabout for generations of educators who have been socialized to do just the opposite. Understanding that their experiences in schools, as in life, may differ significantly from their students is a tension they must learn to hold.

Educators who have made the transition to a structural analysis of inequality possess an advantage in realizing more equitable outcomes, as they are able to focus their energies on interrupting the processes, policies, and practices that contribute to inequitable outcomes. The understanding that systematic failures aren't rooted in biology or culture allows administrators to leverage resources more strategically to effectively address underlying causes.

Teacher practitioners can target their pedagogical approaches in relationship to content they know will resonate with their students or directly address community concerns, as they will have a better sense of what is likely to be relevant. By being candid about the nature of the society we lived in, teachers can help students understand the relationship between what they are studying and the broader implications for life beyond the classroom walls.

This does not mean however, subjecting your students to an endless cavalcade of horrors, or reminding them daily that they are oppressed. Not only are they keenly aware of this fact, they have also spent a lifetime developing compensatory skills and strategies to help navigate their experiential reality and maintain a sense of dignity. Many possess skills and ways of understanding the world we may have never had the need or opportunity to develop.

People develop knowledge in relationship to the problems and challenges we are confronted with. Talented practitioners leverage this knowledge to develop curricular journey that help illuminate how these systems and structures of oppression function, but also to offer examples of how others have challenged such systems throughout time.

Working with this knowledge, educators can create interactive, constructivist, learning environments that recognize and intentionally seek to mobilize the totality of the intellectual and cultural assets present in the environment. Such spaces offer a direct refutation to performative educational spaces that reinforce the racist and maladaptive belief that a singular way of knowing and navigating the world is superior to the others. When educators develop the understanding that learning is a natural process and that intellect is equally ascribed across human populations, they can predictably create inviting learning environments, ones that align their intentions with their practice and ultimately their outcomes.

This is deeply cognitive work, rather than an attitudinal adjustment. It can't happen overnight, as making the pivot isn't an event. The deeper relational contingencies between simplistic understanding of race and the intellectual formations they inform take time to shift. The shift can be an emotionally freighted process as well.

However, the decision to avoid the discomfort of transformation should be understood as being made at the expense of those who do not have the luxury of sidestepping the conversation. Children are required by law to be in schools, as the adults in the room, the ones being compensated to shepherd their development we share a moral and professional obligation to be the most effective practitioners we can possibly be. Not only do our students require this of us, so too does our fractured nation.

ENGAGING WITH THE PAST TO
ILLUMINATE THE PRESENT

Schools don't exist in isolation; they reflect the larger values of a society and often serve the role of inculcating those values for better or worse. To that extent, schools are sites of racialization in the role they fulfill as institutions of nation building. Historically, they have dutifully served the role of providing the structure and systems to bring immigrants, and new generations of residents into the American family. They have policed the language practices and ratified the knowledge claims of each students, assuring that they aligned with the dogmas of the dominant class.

Our public school system is a remarkable institution, a national investment that is profoundly emblematic of the shared aspirations of democracy, though not one without flaws. One would be remiss to not acknowledge that schools have also functioned as diviners of opportunity, somehow magically determining who would be most fit for the high-paying jobs, jobs of the mind if you will, and who would be more suited for jobs of toil and labor. They have functioned as incubators of white supremacy and other notions that seek to normalize subordination as well. They continue this task even in the present.

We can certainly link the past to the present by examining the rhetorical framing emerging from our current level of political dysfunction and civic discord. Pundits, everyday citizens and policy wonks are often heard decrying, "this isn't us" in response to political statements and transgressive policies. Some of the more repugnant statements or political efforts are equated with those of the Nazis, a familiar trope often utilized to heighten a sense of urgency, but also out of desire to distance the nation from the vulgar, inhumane, and indecent consequences of those efforts.

While understandable to some degree, this pattern of affective distancing may provide a modicum of comfort to some, however, it also serves as a disincentive to reckoning. The policies and practices currently being resurrected have precedents in the nation's historical record for anyone wishing to venture to time to explore; they are more American than apple pie. American democracy and racism have always been comfortable bedfellows. To construct understandings of nationhood that disregard this basic fact is narrowly self-serving and dangerous.

Many of the practices and structures we associate with our public school system were developed in the late nineteenth to early twentieth centuries, during the height of the eugenics movement, a scientific and social movement devoted to race betterment, and social efficiency. Many of the assumptions promulgated by these social engineers undergird the foundational infrastructure of education and continue to inform current practice and policy.

A deeper explication of this history will reveal that eugenicists and their backers conceived of the nation as a biological or racial community and that the nation's future was dependent upon the cultivation of the best human stock (Terman 1916, 91–92). Though not unique to the United States, it is important to situate the United States as the leader and chief promulgator of this movement. As educators, we must also understand the centrality of schools as primary sites of eugenic investment and promotion.

It is noteworthy that the majority of the movement's founders and advocates were well to do, white Anglo-Saxon Protestant men, as their assessment
of what constituted the "best stock" can't be divorced from who they were
and the societal positions they occupied. Their deep intellectual commitments
to promulgating their doctrine were messianic. They approached their cause
like the prophets of a new religion (Stoskopf 2002, 69). They sought to have
their dogma function as incontestable truth. To say they were successful in
their endeavor would be an understatement.

Most people can, upon prompting, articulate many, if not most of their
core beliefs. Far fewer could trace the origins of these beliefs or understand
their centrality in the development of the systems in which they serve daily
or the degree to which they continue to be leveraged to normalize racialized
or otherwise unjust outcomes.

Among the ideas generating the most significant appeal and having enduring consequence on education were the beliefs that intellect was fixed rather
than malleable, that intellect was heritable, and that there were innate differences in intellectual capacity within the human family that were ascribed
along lines of race, class, and gender. In order to advance these beliefs,
eugenicists developed disciplinary tools and pedagogical investments to
prove their point.

The origins of statistics, psychometrics, and mental testing, as academic
disciplines were part of this movement, as was the development of the notion
of IQ (Kamin 1974, 5–12). This doctrine is deeply imbedded in the language,
thought patterns, and basic daily functions of educational institutions, even
though the intellectual foundations and social context out of which these
ideas emerged have been thoroughly disproved.

Eugenics was a popular movement that had adherents across the political spectrum. The Progressive Era was a utopian movement that imagined
improving society through advances in science, even as their scientific methods were crude. Progressives were deeply invested in eugenics. The idea that
one could improve society by attending to the human stock had great appeal
and continues to curry favor. At the time of its emergence, most people still
were fairly intimately connected or certainly familiar with the food production cycle. Consequently, the idea that the same kind of procreative manipu-
lation of husbandry that could be achieved with plants and animals could be
applied to the human species was compelling, it made perfect sense.

People then, as now, were enamored with the growing preeminence of
science, the comfort it offered and the promises of certainty it held. The
notion of applied science as an efficient solution to human problems, was
wholly consistent with the notions of scientific promise being promulgated
at the time. Its apparent objectivity and lack of sentimentality also held great
appeal.

Past efforts touting the benefits of increased efficiency and productivity were aggressively promoted by eugenic advocates, often utilizing similar rhetorical patterns of overpromising we witness today by the tech industry. Similar to tech today, the movement was also fairly homogeneous, with little to no representation of the very folks who would bear the brunt of these social engineers' zeal to improve society. Among the problems they were most concerned with was the erosion of the nation's human stock due to the increasing number of immigrants arriving to the country and their expanding presence in the nations' school systems.

Progressive educators were quick to apply this new knowledge. Often school administrators partnered with university faculty to implement new research discoveries, such as in the use of IQ testing. It is important to note the San Francisco Bay Area played a particularly important role in the development of IQ testing and district-wide approaches to mass assessment. Oakland Unified, San Jose Unified, and Palo Alto Unified School districts were among the nation's first districts to embrace these practices (Chapman 1988, 107–27).

The reverence for the work of these men—they were almost exclusively white men engaged in the IQ movement—is borne out by their names gracing the edifices of educational institutions across the region. We can find similar patterns of honorific appellation around the nation, especially in close proximity to the elite universities that enthusiastically promulgated these ideas. However, the espousal of eugenic ideology wasn't limited to elite universities. Eugenics and related courses were a staple offering in nearly two-third of university course catalogues nationally in addition to being present in 90 percent of high school biology textbooks in use up to 1940 as determined by a recent analysis (Haller 1965, 64; Selden 1999, 64).

It is during that time that we see the emergence of language of biological essentialism gaining traction in educational nomenclature and generating shifts in practice. Prior to the advance of eugenics, teachers approached the classroom differently. Tasked with the development of their students, teachers paid close attention to the needs of their students and made informed adjustments, according to what they actually observed and had come to know through their daily interactions.

Though education prior to the rise of eugenics certainly wasn't any Shangri-La, the growing prominence of scientific experts, intelligence metrics, and the rise of social efficiency movements, shifted and in many respects, undermined the role of educator. The context-specific knowledge of their students, the ability to make learning relevant, and the wisdom gleaned through practice became subservient to the knowledge of the experts.

As the influence of IQ testing and other forms of quantification began to take hold, schools began to track students into different categories based on their "innate" ability as determined by the tests. The shift from imagining students as all having potential to grow and make contributions to their communities became a casualty of biological essentialist thinking.

These shifts in thinking not only transformed and diminished the role of the teacher as skilled practitioners, responsible for continual development of their craft, but also transformed them into agents of research institutions and related outside influences that envisioned schools as laboratories for societal betterment. Eugenicists needed to partner with schools in order to advance their agendas as schools were where future generation began their journey. Schools were the seedbeds of the nation.

It bears noting that eugenicists, among others were concerned about the shifting nature of society. By the late nineteenth and early twentieth century the rapid pace of industrialization, national expansion, and larger geopolitical forces generated a new wave of human migration. Many immigrants came to the United States seeking economic opportunity, religious freedom, and freedom from oppression.

These immigrants were not of the traditional WASP stock, increasingly they came from Southern and Eastern Europe. They also came from Asia, Latin America, and other parts of the globe. The presence of growing numbers of European immigrants, who were seen as far from white, generated fears of racial degeneration, amalgamation, and cultural loss. Their whiteness may have been salient in relationship to African Americans, Native Americans, Chinese, and Mexicans who were already present, but they were not seen as fully white, nor were they seen as desirable.

In spite of the deeply held belief that these migrants were racial contaminants, many appeared close enough to passing to pose a threat; specifically the threat of co-mingling their gametes with those of the stock already present. The fears of racial amalgamation became a companion and volatile bedfellow to the growing economic insecurity. The escalating fear that these newer immigrants, viewed as distinct and subordinate races, would take jobs away from folks already here, usurping those more deserving, more "fit," generated the impetus to delineate efficiently and effectively, if not dispassionately. Schools played an increasingly important role in these processes of identification, designation, and delineation.

As changes in the mode of production occurred, the increasing desire to make distinctions between those who should be engaged in the more desirable and lucrative jobs of the mind from those who were to work with their hands took hold (Chapman 1988, 108–9). This process of identification, categorization, and stratification could be most effectively achieved by schools; they were ideally situated to serve this function for the nation. This is the task they still serve today.

As we hear the growing chorus of nativist sentiment and continue to labor under some of the same disruptive economic, social, and political challenges generated by a similar shift in the mode of production as past generations, we must insure that we do not replicate historical patterns of policies rooted in racial nationalist sentiment. In order to interrupt the cycle we must engage with this history and the commitments it engendered. Without a sustained, critical, confrontation with this history we stand little chance, but to repeat it.

An examination of the news cycle over the past several years reveals that this process of repeating our past seems underway. Historically contextualizing our work as educators and functionaries within the educational system, will help to clarify the scope of our efforts as well as to illuminate sites of intervention.

It should also help to clarify that effectively addressing these issues will require long-term strategic approaches that may ultimately take decades to fully implement. Our efforts to resist the educational legacies of these ideas must shift from episodic to sustained confrontation, from more tactical, disjointed approaches toward coordinated, strategic engagement. Attending to these challenges can no longer be viewed as peripheral to the process of education, they must be situated centrally within our work, the health and sustainability of our democracy depends on it.

URGENCY VERSUS TRUE PACE OF CHANGE

There are natural and in many respects, unresolvable tensions we have to brook as educators. The sense of urgency to resolve the challenges we face is unrelenting and yet change takes place in real time. Effective and sustainable efforts toward transformation require developing a sense of shared understanding of the problem among the change makers, developing the capacity and skills necessary to address the range of issues we are confronted with and ultimately leveraging these new understandings to retool or abolish destructive practices in order to systematically replace them with more generative, inclusive, student-centered approaches to learning.

True change also requires developing broader conception of education as living beyond the walls of the school building. Schools that serve the community must engage not only educators and students, but also parents and the broader community in a reciprocal relationship of shared edification.

Even the most effective efforts will not ultimately solve the challenges we face, they are protean in nature, constantly evolving. Their depth and complexity, institutional inertia, and habits of mind, combined with ongoing practices of racial formation will defy the tenure of one's professional career. That doesn't mean we should become apathetic or fall into despair, but rather recalibrate our expectations. We can, through time, clarity of purpose, refinement of practice, alter our practice such that we more predictably create generative, safe, inclusive, vibrant spaces of learning that function as crucibles of civic foment and democracy.

Admittedly, the pace of change often feels too slow; glacial at times. The patterns of failure; attrition, push outs, discipline-based purges, and the inability to effectively shepherd so many of our students through the trajectory of their educational odyssey can be soul crushing. These patterns exist in large part because we are often repeating the same cycles of practice we inherited. Seemingly novel approaches are nevertheless predicated on the same problematic assumptions we seek to confront.

The longer one serves in education, the more evident these pedagogical rotations become. The sort of transformation necessary to interrupt these destructive cycles will require long form solutions both within schools and strategic responses to the forces external to schools that too often drive our practice. We must also realize that we're not simply working to eradicate the legacies of the past, but working to battle new forms and processes of racialization, classification, and subjugation that are currently being enacted (Lipsitz 2019, 40–41).

It is evident in today's political climate, that we don't currently possess the political will to galvanize the public's support in this effort, but we must work with the assumption that a time will come when that political will does galvanize. However, we must not assume it will appear magically, like some apparition. It could emerge out of pragmatic necessity or interest conversion, as demographic shifts make more evident the broader civic, economic, and political consequences of our educational system's failure, though this should not be taken for granted.

The change should be cultivated from within our classrooms through the content we engage our students with, the pedagogical approaches we use, and the questions we ask them to reckon with guided by our understanding of the long-term implications and practical relevance of their constructed knowledge. Our practice must prepare all of our students for this moment and in fact, help them develop the skills and dispositions to shape its emergence.

Additionally, our approaches must address the fundamental reality that their needs, understandings, and eventual application of their learning will necessarily differ as a function of the differential historical legacies and social positioning they inherit, as well as the times in which they live. We certainly can't wait around for things to change, as an absence of action is unacceptable, and immoral. We must not forget that how we go about fomenting change matters.

As educational leaders the desire to act, to do something, comes at the expense of doing things well or even asking the most basic question of why we are doing what we are doing in the first place. Those we hope to serve are too often the victims of these well intended, but not deeply thought through efforts. Simple fixes or quick solutions will never effectively address the challenges we face. The systems we push against are complex, deeply entrenched, and well buttressed by unrelenting forces external to and from within the systems themselves. Knowledge of these dynamics differs across communities leaving many educators ignorant to the forces themselves.

The frenetic nature of educational change efforts is evident in the waves of reform that crash down on our schools with relentless monotony. Some, like Common Core are large, weighty, time-consuming endeavors that promote big shifts in curricular practice and assessment, but eventually wane in significance or continuity under contestation. Similarly, heuristics such as the culture of poverty, colorblindness, and uncritical notions of equal educational access are attractive to many and quickly garner attention.

However, abstracted from the historical policies, practices, and ideological commitments that served to generate the patterns of inequality we presently witness, these intellectual frameworks often bolster and perpetuate, rather than interrupt these patterns (Lipsitz 2019, 41–42). Newer emerging frameworks such as grit, trauma informed practice, zero tolerance, mindset, cultural competence, culturally responsive teaching, and emphasizing empathy are too quickly embraced and uncritically advanced, too often codifying problematic racialized assumptions that serve to entrench the dynamics or become an impediment to meaningful reform.

These initiatives fail to provide relief and uplift for our most marginalized students for two primary reasons. The first and perhaps most difficult to resolve is that too often, the efforts themselves are predicated on the assumed deficiency of certain groups of students, their communities or caregivers.

The failure to question these assumptions or one's relationship to the narratives that produce these understandings tends to generate approaches that target tertiary symptoms of disenfranchisement rather than the structural and ideological commitments driving the malignant and demoralizing outcomes. Additionally, practitioners also fail to question these basic assumptions of deficiency and may in fact believe them themselves, consciously or otherwise (Eberhardt 2005, 182).

This failure to reflect on our larger societal patterns and our complicity in reproducing them encourages educators to seek "quick fixes" that too often end up collapsing or corrupting useful pedagogical approaches and innovations reducing their potential impact or transforming them into intention-driven rationalizations or defenses of bad practice. The desire to implement too quickly or to simplify complex ideas often reduces the potential efficacy of these approaches or divorces them from the original intent. The pressure to meet short-term performance goals encourages embracing and abandoning tactics in a serial fashion, rather than developing long-term strategic approaches that could be aligned, integrated, and effectively coalesced to amplify impact.

Effective leadership can temper and direct that sense of urgency by creating structured opportunities that assist the community in developing a unified conception of the challenges faced, that increase the community's capacity to effectively address those challenges and, over time, systematize these new understandings and approaches. Such efforts can increase a sense of shared endeavor, collective agency and uplift, generating not just knowledge of how to promote effective reform, but also the necessary will.

RESISTANCE AS SELF-PROTECTION

To be clear, not all students embrace these performances of knowledge. The range of responses can vary significantly. How we as educators interpret these responses and respond to them can have enduring consequences for our students. Consequences that can affirm, embolden, and stoke critical thinking among students, inviting them into a lifelong quest for understanding. Our responses can also silence, stifle, and chasten their curiosity, rendering the classroom a space of resistance, and self-protection, producing an intellectual and civic dead zone.

Some students choose to actively resist and to confront these processes directly. Too often, these efforts toward self-protection are misinterpreted and met with institutional power instead of being seen for what they are. Rather than interpreting this resistance as a form of critical thinking or self-protection and engaging these students dialectically, too frequently the desire to avoid tension leads to the removal of these students from the classroom.

Not only do these efforts inflict direct harm on the questioning student, these patterns of interaction can also stifle others and further erode the vitality of the learning space. Were teachers to engage, rather than to avoid these moments, they would be far more likely to keep that particular student connected to the learning process, but also bring others along to probe and explore more deeply.

Racial disparities in disciplinary data serve as an additional body of evidence that speaks to this reality, especially when considering the degree to which defiance is cited as a basis for disciplinary action. Not all students have the capacity to resist, some may simply whither under these circumstances and surrender.

The sense that the game is rigged against them and not likely to change, unfortunately causes many students to give up their voice or interest in learning, as least in a formal sense. Students in these situations often find more value in maintaining a sense of dignity and humanity than engaging with presentations of self or community that are demoralizing and dehumanizing. The decision to opt out of a system one has been socialized to see as essential is a powerful act of critical thinking, if not a bit maladaptive.

The work of Claude Steele and other researchers of stereotype threat can also provide fertile ground for exploration for anyone interested in gaining a deeper understanding of how issues of identity related to historically constructed notions of ability can wreak havoc in the relationally transactive space of the classroom. *Whistling Vivaldi* would be my suggested place to begin this journey. This body of research surfaces important insights that reveal learning isn't simply an act of producing or performing knowledge.

The growing body of evidence suggests, among other things, that the classroom space isn't neutral or universally experienced. Classrooms are not environments in which all identities are similarly positioned and treated as having equal value or worth, contrary to colorblind socialization. Far from being a place of equal educational opportunity, a notion to which many educators subscribe, it is a place sedimented with the detritus of historically generated and contemporarily produced racialized tropes, practices, and policies (Gordon 2019, 227–31).

The weight of centuries of racialization, much of which has been obscured or minimized, creates an asymmetrical playing field in which historically marginalized groups continue to be measured against the standpoint of white normativity. Evaluated primarily on the basis to which they conform to and perform these patterns of cognition without resistance or contention, success is a complicated and not without consequences.

The psycho-social repercussions of identity threat aren't solely borne by marginalized communities. Students and educators who identify as white are also part of this complex mix of relational interactions. Socialization into whiteness comes at a cost in these diverse relational ecosystems. Whether framed as conceptual impoverishment, affective under-skilling, or white fragility, the inability to comprehend the possibility of different understandings of the world or to hold the dissonance that is typically generated when confronted with these, often novel understandings has significant ramifications.

Revanchist responses of hostility, reassertion of white normativity, and expressions of disapproval surface with frequency, distancing white identifying educators and students from their colleagues of color and their knowledge. These fractures separate educators from the relationships and understanding they need to effectively situate themselves within a more accurate, comprehensive, and ultimately more cognitively generative, and civically useful understanding of the world (Reynolds 2019, 354–59). They need to be able to inhabit this space in order to create the same for their students.

As leaders we can begin to shift these dynamics by reimagining the curricular journey and expanding beyond the well-defined boundaries and cultural frameworks that privilege certain histories, and experiences to the exclusion of others. As our classrooms reflect the growing diversity of our nation, so too should the curriculum and modes of interaction. Constructing relevant and reflective content can facilitate higher levels of engagement for marginalized student populations, but the benefit of such shifts is larger. Such content can also introduce counternarratives that reflect different understandings of the world, understandings of equal relevance, and utility.

The fact that one can pass through our educational system and be considered well educated without ever having to engage, in substantial ways with the history, literature, political, or creative contributions of so many of their fellow citizen's contributions to this nation is frankly criminal. These patterns of diminution by omission serve to skew the value not only of knowledge, but also of the people producing it. In this current moment, the consequences of such approaches are revealing themselves to constitute a threat to our democracy.

With growing interest in the development of ethnic studies courses and newly revised history and social studies standards we a have a solid foundation to build upon. We can use these structures to cultivate higher levels of engagement among our students, but also use them to cultivate a more critical sense of civic agency.

There is great potential in utilizing these new frameworks to construct an intellectual scaffold that will promote a more complex understanding of comparative racialization. Doing so would require reframing or complicating more traditional multicultural survey approaches to ethnic studies. This is not to suggest that a reflective and representational approach is no longer warranted, but in order to illuminate the power dynamics, ideological drivers, and continuities of these processes, it is important to revise our approach.

Such efforts could facilitate a more nuanced and historically accurate understanding that all groups are racialized, not just BIPOC. This pivot is necessary to disrupt the normalizing social hierarchies. It is entirely possible to speak of identity and different experiences of group identity without ever picking up on the purposes and processes of identification; this needs to change.

We can witness the stultifying consequences of this framing nearly each day as media pundits, politicians, and citizens alike struggle to make meaning of the current moment. The sort of mental gymnastics of justification, we see from the political left and right provide a consistent stream of evidence that addressing past and present patterns of inequality through simplification, omission, and aspirations alone will not develop the necessary insights or skills necessary to shepherd us safely and collectively into the future.

A CALL FOR RECKONING

Surveys of student performance data by subject area may offer some additional evidence to these dynamics. In examining achievement gaps—a term worthy of some interrogation—by subject, the gap tends to be the smallest in math, gets larger in literature, and is the largest in history (Loewen and Sebesta 2011, 20). This suggests that the content itself, especially as it functions as a mirror on students' lived realities, can be a site of conflict and contestation (Loewen 2018, 10–17).

Subject matter that could be a source of sustenance, affirmation, and civic contemplation, too often becomes weaponized or pacifying, damaging minoritized students and white students alike. Efforts to avoid possible conflict or discomfort or that simply reflect a teacher's own lack of knowledge, serve to impoverish students' sense of democratic possibility. By papering over past efforts to secure justice, dignity, humanity, and democracy from the hands of tyranny, white supremacy and patriarchy, we divorce the study of history and the humanities from their purpose.

Too often lost in these efforts to secure comfort are the stories of those who could see beyond their present moment, those who embraced solidarity, struggle and a sense of shared destiny. The nation has survived times far more volatile and violent than our present one, we must not forget that. Even in the worst of times there were those who stood up, challenged the norms, and demanded more from our country. These are among the stories we need to reclaim.

As it becomes more evident that many have lost their sense of democratic imagination, much of which seems to be tied to different understandings of our past, these stories can provide a source of nourishment for our civic imagination. I am not suggesting that surfacing these stories alone will be sufficient, as there are no singular or simple solutions to the issues we face. However, it is clear, that without engaging more critically and inclusively with our past history we will struggle to forge a path forward as a collective.

In a moment in which trigger warnings, noncritical frameworks of safety, and empathy are being advanced to reassert the primacy of white normativity in educational spaces, we need to remain cognizant that learning isn't simply a performative act limited to academic success and ascension. Students need, and will be compelled to apply their knowledge or lack thereof, across a variety of domains after exiting the classroom.

Preparing them to meet that challenge should be among our top priorities (Sensoy and DiAngelo 2014, 1–10). The domains of application are neither static, nor they time-bound, consequently, cultivating intellectual habits of mind that fall short of equipping students to face these tribulations, does those students and society a grave disservice.

The failure to appreciate the complexity of these issues generates patterns of civic assertion that serve to reproduce preexisting inequalities rather than to eradicate them. It becomes increasingly important to grapple with the fact that business as usual will not prepare our students for the more diverse future they will inhabit. This is increasingly apparent for white identifying students, as the historical legacies of our nation's commitment to racial segregation and presentations of their experiences as universal, leave them ill prepared for the current and emerging demographic landscape of our nation, one which will surely become more diverse. Intermarriage, internal birthrates, and the broader implications of climate change fueled migration will ensure as much.

The degree to which these changes will shape our nation are hard to imagine, but that is what we must do. More importantly, we must invite our students to do so as well. Schools need to become an integral part of this larger process of societal transformation, especially in regard to elucidating the positive aspects of this transformation. Change is not without challenge, but it is also not without tremendous possibility. Schools should invite students into this conversation sooner rather than later.

EDUCATION FOR LIBERATION

Emancipatory education requires anticipating the various contexts in which our students will apply their learning. Our increasingly mobile lifestyle will necessitate students' developing the ability to navigate different contexts throughout their lives and work careers. Our society, like others, is in a constant state of evolution and will remain so.

A proper education should reflect that reality. We can't prepare them by selectively presenting the past, choosing to focus primarily on the positive and seemingly redeeming moments, we must engage with it all; the good, bad, and the wretched. This more comprehensive reckoning is required to help elucidate how patterns of the past are being reconstituted, reproduced, and reasserted. The ideological drivers of difference assure that students need to be flexible in their thinking such that they can hold complexity as well as contradictions.

They will need to be able to inhabit different understandings of the world simultaneously. To imagine themselves as somewhat fluid, existing within the ever-evolving relational ecosystem of our nation or where ever they may choose to reside, rather than static, geographically bound, essentialized entities incapable of change.

Our persistent patterns of educational segregation present a challenge to this goal. It is difficult to fully comprehend who we are as a nation, let alone our roles within it without sustained engagement across perceived or real markers of difference. An education that doesn't prepare all students for this reality is ineffective, unethical, and frankly dangerous in a society freighted with, and buttressed by unequal power relationships.

To the extent that classrooms are a microcosm of society, it is an ideal place to cultivate these competencies. The asymmetries of power, knowledge, access to material resources among other markers of status and membership are present in any classroom, as they are in the rest of society. So too do the bubbles of isolation exist within education. Tracking and scheduling among other institutional practices almost insure that students inhabiting different neighborhoods, socioeconomic environments, and speaking different home languages will be invariably traveling different, if not parallel paths during their education. The opportunity to transcend the artificially imposed markers of worth rarely surface.

Inviting students to openly and intentionally interrogate these power dynamics is necessary for schools to be a place of relevance, importance, and challenge for all students. Educators interested in co-creating emancipatory classrooms with their students should also share a disposition of inquiry, intellectual curiosity combined with a willingness to sit with uncertainty.

A learning environment that typifies these norms will likely elicit high levels of engagement and at times conflict, as that is a given when encouraging students to coalesce differences of opinion and understanding, especially when they are authentically reflective of our different lived experiences. We should challenge the notion that the discomfort that comes with challenging beliefs and complicating thinking is inherently bad, or to be avoided.

Social and emotional learning should be integrated into all the work we do, not positioned as an enhancement, a pull out or something ancillary to the core curriculum. With deeper knowledge of our students and the communities they come from, teachers can develop curricular journeys, undergirded by thoughtful pedagogical choices to create opportunities for learning that are affectively and cognitively beneficial. Learning to hold dissonance and embrace tension are essential elements of critical thinking and effective civic participation.

Schools should be among the places where these competencies are nurtured and cultivated. As such, learning should not be constrained solely to the physical sites of schools, it needs to be connected to the larger community. Learning should not just be about community it should include community.

Deeper exploration of the varying local contexts should illuminate opportunities for engagement, support, and service, mechanisms through which students can develop a sense of agency, purpose, and connection. Reimagining schools as places where we reclaim the intimacy of connection, of relationships is within our realm of possibility. This must be central to our focus, as the work of rebuilding coherence and a sense of shared purpose within our nation will require nothing less.

SCHOOLS AS RELATIONAL ECOSYSTEMS

Relationships matter. Getting to know one's students isn't a quick fix or a tactic, but rather is a foundational necessity to effectively engage your students. Making the time to cultivate these connections serves the teacher and student alike and can enhance overarching learning objectives. Learning is a social, relational act not simply an individual one. Viewed from this vantage point, the production of knowledge is a process of co-construction rather than competition as it is too frequently implied (Steele and Cohn-Vargas 2013, 6–11).

If understood as such, focusing on the quality of the relationships between teachers and students, the students with each other, and the parents with the school may be among the most important places to invest in our practice. Schools, like other institutions are relational ecosystems. When those systems are healthy, students can devote more attention to learning and knowledge production than to vigilance (Steele 2010, 124–27).

The axiom that our students will learn more for us than from us rings largely true. Cultivating a sense of learning as shared endeavor is likely more consistent with our students' lived experiences. This may be especially true of marginalized students, as communal collaboration may be the only means of survival available in environments noted more for unpredictability, uncertainty, disruption and privation than the gentile suburbs their teachers are likely to hail from.

Our ability as educational leaders to develop communities of practice that express explicitly and implicitly that we value our students, their families, and the communities we serve, that we truly see them, can help mitigate school's negative impacts on learning, a natural, otherwise organic process. Operating is this capacity, schools can also provide a space of refuge and security from the tumult, turbulence, and lack of predictability of the larger society.

Our ability to curate a relevant and meaningful educational journey can only come from engaging with our students, understanding what is important to them, and what the issues or concerns are that occupy their minds. While these efforts will not necessarily directly address the larger institutional practices and ideologies that drive problematic outcomes, they can increase the likelihood that educators, students, and parents, engage as meaningful partners in a process of shared edification, mitigating some routines and habits that thwart such alliances.

The pivot from understanding education as primarily an individual act of striving or performance toward a more relational approach to learning also has implications for how we as educational leaders think about parent engagement. Ideally, educators and parents are in a partnership, one focused on the needs of the students, but also connected to the broader community concerns and needs.

The investment of time and resources to create a broader sense of shared enterprise with parents is very worthwhile. At a minimum, authentic efforts to engage parents and to communicate they are an essential part of the learning partnership helps build trust. Trust is an essential foundation of learning and collaborative processes. Deeper connections with parents can exponentially expand the capacity of schools to meet their broader educational mission by leveraging parental expertise, cultural assets, and knowledge of community.

Cultivating these parental relationships provides us with deeper knowledge not only of community needs, but also of its aspirations. Think of this process as a form of courtship in which we, as representative of the institutions we serve, make sure we are on our best behavior, that we demonstrate our commitment through flexibility and accommodation. In most cases, this means being open about when we set meetings times, where we set them, whether we bring in translators, or provide child care, food, and much more.

In essence, we must invest in systematized caring, though never allowing it to become transactional. These investments pay dividends when given proper attention and structured into the normative practices of schools. Structural integration of caring needs to become part and parcel of everything we do. It should inform how we hire, how we transition students and families into our community, and also in how we celebrate our successes and face the challenges that inevitably surface over the course of any given school year. Building equity in these relationships will also allow us to make the occasional withdrawal when needed, often with much less strife.

A NECESSARY SHIFT IN PERSPECTIVE

One way to disrupt the predictability of our educational systems' outcomes is to question the framing of the discourse. We tend to approach solutions in relationship to how we define the challenges we face. A pivot to reconsider the narrative of failure may be necessary to fully comprehend the scope of work that lies ahead.

Attention to this shift will necessitate accounting for teachers' generational socialization into "colorblind" teaching practice. However well intentioned, which it likely is for many educators, the idea of people convincing themselves they don't see color, or any difference for that matter, in a society that has deep intellectual, structural, and material investments in constructing difference is profoundly maladaptive. It is also historically abstractive. We can't fundamentally see our students, meet their needs, or stand any chance to offering a transformative education without acknowledging this reality.

The rush to anoint the nation "post-racial" immediately following the election of President Barack Obama offers us a case in point. That narrative, one promulgated by many progressive educators, required dismissing an abundance of evidence to the contrary, even as Obama's runup to the 2009 election was taking place. Utterly consistent with our nation's ethos of individual merit and the redeeming capacity of American democracy, his election, for many, signaled the end of our nation's struggle with racism.

The triumph of the Civil Rights era was finally manifest in the inauguration of President Obama, or so it seemed. Admittedly, it was difficult not to be moved by his election, though much easier to not get swept up in the celebratory chorus. It had been easier to imagine the election of a woman as president than to entertain the possibility of electing a person of color during the course of my lifetime. Born to a father, who was raised in the Jim Crow south, his election existed as an unrealistic probability, nearly an impossibility. It wasn't until a few days after the fact, my father accepted the election outcome as real.

However, it was also clear that Obama's election, in no way, signaled the end to our nation's preoccupation with race. Far from it. Even as many were celebrating, others saw this same inauguration as the beginning of the end, a signal that the nation was soon to be lost. With both sentiments clearly present, how was it that so many failed to hold the contradictions of the moment and to wrestle with what those contradictions might mean for the nation? Unfortunately, it didn't take long for the insidious forces of racism to stoke divisions and discord, these forces are with us, gaining momentum, and are likely to be something we'll have to contend with for the foreseeable future. Why did so many, fail to see this coming?

Undergirding this process was an uncritical embrace of the notion of universalism of identity. Perhaps rooted in a prosocial aspiration to live in a society in which all people are treated fairly and equally, one where individuals rise or fall based on their own efforts. This framing obscures historical reality and becomes an impediment to seeing things as they are. Unfortunately, aspirations, abstracted from a historical understanding of the processes and policies of categorical identification, will likely lead to more entrenched inequity. Too often, this framing leads educators of progressive inclinations to focus on defending their intentions when called to task about the impact of their actions.

It is difficult to explore issues of power, positionality, or the fact that categorical classifications have enduring material consequences by focusing primarily on individual experiences or stories. Yes, they can provide us with some powerful and often useful insights into individual experiences, however not without a cost. The framing of individual identity as opposed to collective identification is a central tactic of white supremacy.

The narrow focus thwarts interrogation of the larger societal factors that inform these experiences. This process of decontextualization feeds habits of mind that can lead to victim blaming and serve larger objectives presenting inequality as natural, eroding civic efforts to challenge inequitable outcomes. The legacies of these patterns of historical classification have to be of primary concern. Schools have functioned as sites of identification, categorization, classification, and stratification from their inception. They continue to execute this function presently. We have to understand this reality in order to interrupt it.

Generating more equitable and less predictably racialized outcomes, can only happen through a sustained confrontation with white supremacy and it's first cousin colorblind ideology. Decades of defining racism and other forms of categorical oppression narrowly as overt, intentional acts perpetrated by individuals, rather than the manifestation of ideologically driven institutional violence, has left most people ill equipped to understand the complexity of these dynamics. Without a nuanced, historically rooted, comprehension of these issues, effective intervention is impossible, reproduction becomes the norm, almost an inevitability.

Colorblind investments also become an impediment to making classrooms a place of transformation, as curricular journeys curated from this standpoint will likely miss opportunities to explore how difference is constructed, not to mention the consequences of these constructions. To the extent that an overarching goal of colorblindness is to avoid addressing difference, the contributions of those representing different experiences will be devalued or avoided all together.

The presence and absence of particular experiences in the classroom communicate powerful messages about who and what is seen as important or relevant and who or what is not. Teachers can't teach what they don't know. As such, an essential requirement for teaching in this moment and toward a shared future necessitates teachers themselves, become learners and excavators of histories, histories they themselves have been systematically denied access to (Loewen 2018, 17–19).

Failure to commit to this path of conceptual expansion prevents the development of a more critically useful intellectual framework or scaffold of knowledge, one that has the capacity to develop in complexity and utility over time. A lack of historical understanding also truncates one's civic imagination.

One can't envision a world different from the one we inhabit without interrogating the ideas that generate the impoverishing patterns we've been conditioned to see as rooted in failures of biology or behavioral decisions. Such constructions discourage exploration of the robust possibilities of an inclusive democratic society. Sparking historical imagination requires asking the "what if" questions of our past, but also of our present and future. Imagination is the catapult to possibility.

Most people, including educators, inhabit all too comfortably pathologizing narratives that juxtapose the gentile suburbs as sites of meritocratic endeavor against squalid urban communities. Accused of lacking care for their community, being lazy, or failing to make better life choices, these assumptions are difficult to transcend. Absent cognition of the role our Federal Government and banking institutions played in generating these material asymmetries, it is difficult to understand these dynamics or disentangle the related assumptions from the mental maps formed around the omission of these historical facts.

These structural, policy-based commitments impact educational funding along with access to other critical resources and opportunities. By situating our practice within this deeper analysis, we can see that educational success isn't just about supporting our students in navigating the educational system, it must also include enhancing their ability to see their efforts and success as a form of direct confrontation with the system itself.

In the current moment, efforts to excavate history critically aren't simply for those who bear its yoke, but for those who may identify more with those applying the yoke. There is increasing evidence, anxiety, depression, suicide, the current opiate addiction crisis, and patterns of violence that suggest the dominant narrative of the world is also unhealthy to those who on the outset may appear to benefit from it. The ability to usurp the function of democracy by appealing to the anxieties and fears that undergird these signs of duress threatens our nation and the ability to effectively govern it. These anxieties are likely to intensify even though at the core they are predicated on lies and half-truths.

The current president's dog whistle to "make America great again" is predicated on a mythical past that assumes that our future is doomed by the demographic transformation of our society. It is as though communities who have long contributed to the success of this country can't possibly shepherd it into a more beautiful and inclusive from of democracy. Lost in this narrative is the uncontestable fact that our democracy is what it is in large part due to the efforts of those who have resisted and fought against dehumanization and subjugation. Those who had the temerity to dream of better times, even when those dreams felt remote.

Our current moment also suggests the need to lift up and elevate the histories of solidarity that have always been part and parcel of our nation's ongoing struggle to create a truly inclusive and just society. Emancipatory education, one that equips students to become agents of societal change isn't an act of charity, but rather an avenue toward collective liberation.

Democracy neither is a zero-sum game, nor has it ever been.

White identifying students are damaged, however differently, by an educational system that promises them perpetual dominance in positionality. That very notion is itself a lie, one nearly as destructive to their wellbeing as it is to those they've been promised positionality over. It is also destructive to the functioning of our democracy, a fact becoming more evident every day. We need not countenance the anxieties, losses, and human wastage caused by allegiance to these limiting narratives, we have a choice to make.

CONCLUSION: VISIONING FORWARD

Our democracy has been improved by the efforts of many who have valiantly waged sustained efforts to make true the promise of our founding documents. Closing the chasm between the articulated values of a democracy—founded during a time of human bondage, dispossession, and genocide of Indigenous communities and consistent subjugation of those racially othered—has always been forwarded by those on the margins. Our history is repeatedly punctuated by moments where groups and individuals have banded together to pursue the imagination of an inclusive society.

In spite of our recurrent patterns fracturing and division, there have always been those among us who knew our best days were ahead of us. That through a sense of shared liberation and a disdain for inequality threw their bodies into the fray to secure a better future. That dream is still alive. The classroom is a place where freedom dreams need to be kindled, stoked, and ignited. This is our work as educators, we are the dream keepers of the nation.

In this current moment we need a bolder vision for education, one that recognizes the gifts and talents of all of our students, the unique knowledge and understanding of the world each of them carries. Realizing this possibility will require engaging with the history of ideas that has been leveraged to deny this basic fact in service of normalizing educational outcomes that denigrate and deny the humanity of an increasing number of our students.

Making these shifts will necessitate a long-term commitment to this work. It took decades to build up the political capital and civic commitments to birth the Civil Rights Movement and other liberation movements, similarly, it took decades of investment to undermine and overturn those gains. The pendulum swings of our democratic spasms are developments not events, our practice as educators must recognize this. The sense of urgency will always be there; the stakes admittedly are high. However, we must not let our desire to perform virtue interfere with doing what's right or necessary to achieve our goals.

The deep and interlocking contingencies of a system built on assumptions about human ability and worth will take significant time and political will to overhaul. We will surely face resistance along the way. Forces from within and outside the system with material investments in status quo will attempt to thwart our efforts, we must resist the desire to succumb to these forces or play nice, we must not be moved.

The problems we face such as climate change, growing economic dispar- ity, and the resurgence of racial nationalism will require our collective efforts and long-term commitments to solve. We can no longer be satisfied with fiddling around the edges of a system that at its core is deeply flawed and in many respects not designed to do what we need it to nor cultivate the skills needed for the work ahead. The changes needed to birth a new vision of education are foundational in nature. We've never had a system that equally invests in the potential of each and every student, yet that is the system we must imagine and then build.

In such a system, learning needs to be connected to the contexts and situa- tions in which knowledge will be applied. It must cultivate the habits of mind that allow students to hold complexity and ambiguity. Similarly, it must also help them develop a sense of agency and the skills to forge community and work collaboratively with others. Learning cannot simply be a performance of "fitness," it must prepare our students to grapple with the challenges we will face as a national and global community.

We will need to steel ourselves and support each other in this work. We are always smarter as a collective, it will be necessary to harness our collective insights and understandings to do this work effectively. We have the power to reimagine schools as intentional communities of caring and connection, where we rejoice in each other's presence and affirm each other's contribu- tions to the collective.

Let us all look forward to the day when self-serving, charity-driven narratives that celebrate the success of the few, that simultaneously serve to countenance the "failure" of the majority, are no longer to be viewed as acceptable—may the notion of a "talented tenth" be relegated to the dustbin of history. When students who resist and question are seen as assets to the collective learning, not those fit for banishment we will be on our way.

When we are able to create schools that are relational ecosystems it will be easier to understand that our destinies are intertwined, that we actually need each other. Liberation in this sense isn't an individual act or an entitlement directed toward any particular group, but rather a collective escape from an oppressive mythology that encourages us to devalue each other and in turn ourselves. We can do better, we must do better. The years ahead aren't only filled with challenge, they are also pregnant with possibility. There is no other group better positioned to help move our nation forward than we are as educators.

We have our work cut out for us, but with clarity, courage and by harnessing the power of the collective, we can get there. There is dignity in struggle, let us embrace it. See you in the trenches!

REFLECTIVE QUESTIONS FOR LEADING
IN THE BELLY OF THE BEAST

1. What would it mean to approach the classroom with the idea that each and every one of our students might be having a different experience rather than assuming that all students are equally positioned and have equal opportunities to succeed?

2. Learning is a process rather than an event. How might our need or desire as educators to help students meet short-term learning objectives interfere with the long-term more existentially rooted aspects of learning? What would it mean to consider that our students' long-term application of their learning or their motivation for learning may differ significantly from ours?

3. The idea of race was developed and promulgated to create scientific justifications for social hierarchies among other things. In this sense, race or more effectively stated racialization is an active, ongoing process. What would it mean to consider that our schools are not broken, but do exactly what they were designed to do? What sort of personal/collective study would be required to reframe your understanding of race as an idea, such that your practice could be reformed to function as a direct repudiation of this deeply embedded, but tragically false narrative?

4. Deep learning and meaning making is as much an affective process as it is a cognitive one. What kind of support would you require and would you need to provide for your staff to develop a pedagogical practice that is as affectively generative as it is cognitively generative? What would that approach look and feel like in increasingly diverse learning environments?

5. Learning is a social act. What would it mean to think about our classrooms or schools as relational ecosystems? How might this framing help us to more effectively engage with and honor the unique attributes that all of our students bring to the table? How might reframing our understanding of success as a collective process, rather than individual acts of striving or "competition" shape our practice and our outcomes?

6. The current political reality as well as the persistent patterns of disparate educational outcomes provide ample evidence that our schools are not meeting the greater needs of society, nor in many respects the students they serve. Over the next few decades climate change fueled patterns of

global migration will likely reconfigure the demographic makeup of all nations. In what ways does your practice help your students develop the skills and competencies that will allow them to thrive and make meaningful contributions to our society? How is the increasing diversity of our classrooms an asset in this process?

7. As career educators we have a unique opportunity to be engaged in a sustained process of learning. What sorts of communities, support systems, knowledge stores, or networks do you belong to or imagine joining to support your learning? If this is not something you've thought about yet, I invite you to meditate on this question. We are always smarter as a collective, what sort of learning communities would you like to join or envision to nurture your ongoing growth as an educator?

Chapter 2

Focus on the Core

Leading toward Community, Solidarity, and Purpose

Trevor Gardner

Community isn't always synonymous with warmth and harmony. Politeness is often a veneer for understanding, when in reality it masks uncovered territory, the unspeakable pit that we turn from because we know the pain and anger that can dwell there. It is important to remind ourselves that real community is forged out of struggle. This is the crucible from which a real community grows.

—Linda Christensen, Reading,
Writing & Rising Up

INTRODUCTION

For those who lead schools in the United States, especially those leading in historically marginalized and under-resourced communities, the following environment is almost certainly familiar:

Around mid-February, you begin to hear rumblings of increasing discontent.

"There is just too much on our plate" becomes a constant refrain. Teachers begin pulling back more frequently from responsibilities. Fewer staff step into voluntary activities such as dances and clubs. Attendance at professional development sessions takes a dip. And for those who attend, the level of engagement sags like a tarp under heavy winter rains. More conflicts arise among and between staff, and staff room conversations become more critical, toxic even. The lull in positive energy becomes palpable, and it is undoubtedly being transferred to students in the classroom.

These conditions and behaviors are not, as the mainstream narrative about schools and teachers may have us believe, the manifestation of uncaring educators[1] who have little investment in the success of their students. They are not the griping of disgruntled teachers who have lost their motivation and sense of purpose. They are not a disorderly or lazy attempt to undermine the goals and mission of our schools. Rather, they are the rational and predictable result of the incessant pressure of working in the belly of the beast.

In order to sustain and for a school to thrive, leaders must remain rooted in a set of mission-focused Core Values and preempt this energy by building and maintaining a collective foundation of community, solidarity, and purpose that helps everyone navigate the complex and demanding challenges that arise when working in such overly burdened and under-resourced conditions.

COMPLEX AND UNRELENTING WORK

Leadership is complex and unrelenting work, under any conditions. But in schools, especially those serving students in historically marginalized and under-resourced communities, the challenge is further complicated by the paradox inherent in the institution of public education.

Schools are expected to take on significant responsibility in "solving" many of society's problems. Poverty, community fragmentation, violence, illiteracy, mental health ailments, minimal access to healthy food, technology addiction, a culture of incarceration—and the corresponding trauma experienced by young people due to these ills—are a few of the issues placed on the shoulders of educators and schools to carry, allowing the broader society (and those in power) to abdicate responsibility for the economic and social reforms necessary for us to collectively thrive.

However, the resources provided to schools to advance a program that adequately and equitably educates young people and prepares them for careers and life in the twenty-first century, a task that inherently requires addressing the trauma related to the social ills identified above, are, by design, insufficient.

Pedro A. Noguera, Professor of Education and Information Studies at UCLA, elucidates this paradox:

> Policy makers have done relatively little to help schools or provide guidance in how they should address rising poverty, homelessness, and hunger. Recognizing the impossibility of separating a child's educational needs from their social,

psychological, and emotional needs, public schools are forced to devise strategies to address the social needs of children who arrive at school poorly nourished, in poor health, lacking adequate housing, and in some cases suffering from various forms of trauma and toxic stress. That they often respond inadequately is as much a testament to the difficulty of the responsibility that has been placed on them as it is to a lack of competence or commitment. (Noguera 2017, 132)

Given this context, school leadership is a Sisyphean endeavor. Even excellent leaders face continual challenges. Beyond the normal dynamics of organizational leadership, the elements beyond their locus of control in schools line up like an army at the gates.

It is not a coincidence that work in schools is often described through a war metaphor: being "in the trenches." It is exhausting—physically, mentally, emotionally, and psychologically. Days are frenetic and expand far beyond the seven or so hours per day educators spend in direct service to their students, engaging them in the learning of their academic subjects.

The brilliant leadership theorist Margaret Wheatley places this dilemma in a broader social context when she posits, "Under the relentless pressure of time vanishing, we are losing many essential capacities of being human: the time to think and reflect, the time to be in relationships, the time to develop trust and commitment. In essence, we are forfeiting our unique human qualities in exchange for speed" (2001).

The combination of overwhelming working conditions and shamefully limited resources lends itself to toxic environments in schools, environments in which, despite the best efforts and relentless work of educators, success is hard to come by. Consequently, it is common for those working in schools to turn on others in their school community, those closest to their daily experience, to find fault.

As Eugene Eubanks, Ralph Parrish, and Diane Smith state in their foundational chapter "Changing the Discourse in Schools":

Urban schools are full of [students who are failed by the system] . . . . We blame each other, we blame "downtown," but mostly we blame the children and their families. We blame everyone and everywhere except where the problem probably largely lies—in a social/economic-cultural system that requires and "needs" to create persons of poverty to preserve a well-protected system of social privilege. (6)

Failure to adequately and equitably educate all students is to successfully maintain the status quo. And schools do this well, year after year, from one generation to the next.

Without a different approach to leadership in schools, one that understands the system not as broken but as functioning successfully, schools will remain as institutions of social reproduction.

Today, a majority of public school students in the United States, roughly 51 percent in 2013 according to the Southern Education Foundation, are considered "low income," qualifying for free and reduced lunch benefits. Given that parental income is the number one indicator for both individual student achievement and school performance, the challenge is pervasive.

How, then, does a leader, in the midst of such demanding conditions defy the status quo and build a school that does actually function to transform the lives of young people, most of whom the system was set up to fail?

CORE VALUES

What do we stand for? What is at the core of our identities as leaders? What guides our decisions, allocation of resources, and prioritization of time and energy? What is the vision we communicate to our staff, students, and communities? The responses to these fundamental questions begins with establishing, honing, and communicating a set of Core Values that keeps leaders rooted in their purpose, values that recognize and empathize with the relentless pressure of work in schools while maintaining the need to always give all that we can and continually innovate in service of our students and communities.

This chapter summarizes how Trevor Gardner, a school leader at small high school in Oakland, California, attempts to find this balance and create the conditions for transformation in the belly of the best.

Gardner is the director of Teaching and Learning at ARISE High School, a small, mission-focused school of about 400 students serving East Oakland's Fruitvale district. ARISE's student population is over 90 percent Latinx and 100 percent students of color, over 90 percent of whom qualify for free and reduced lunch. His students come from many different places, cultures, and histories but where they find common ground is in their belief in education as the path to create better lives for themselves and their families.

Gardner started his career in education as a teacher when he was only twenty-two years old and taught history, English, creative writing, and leadership at four different schools before taking the position at ARISE. After seventeen years of teaching, leaving the classroom was a complicated decision for him. He was the teacher who looked negatively upon, even condemned those who left teaching after only a few years, or who moved from teaching to positions beyond the classroom. He had developed much of his identity, his sense of self, and his consciousness in the classroom, with his students.

So, when he transitioned into a position of leadership, he knew it was essential to maintain his clarity of purpose and he believed that if he communicated this clearly, his staff would have greater respect for him and his position.

Over the course of a few years, as he took on greater leadership at his school, he developed a set of professional Core Values. Though these values were unique to him and his identity as a leader—a middle-class white man[2] who did not grow up in Oakland, leading a school whose student body consisted of 100 percent students of color and whose staff was over two-third educators of color—they were profoundly shaped by multiple influences: the mentors who had guided him since his first day in the classroom, collaboration with organizations such as Facing History and Ourselves, Teachers 4 Social Justice, and the National Equity Project, study of key educational theorists such as Paulo Freire and bell hooks, and participation in critical inquiry groups with other educators equally invested in digging deeply into the challenges of teaching.

These Core Values became the foundation and the moral compass for his leadership:

BOX 2.1 TREVOR GARDNER'S LEADERSHIP CORE VALUES

Urgency and Patience

Educating the youth is one of the most crucial responsibilities in the world. So much is at stake, especially for educators working with communities that have and continue to experience marginalization and oppression. I must bring a sense of urgency to my leadership that recognizes and respects the needs of our students and communities. However, in order to truly serve teachers and my school community, I must meet them where they are at and hold a space for them to grow just as I grow with them. This requires patience. A leader must constantly navigate the tension between urgency and patience.

The Fire

Teachers almost always get into the profession from a place of passion, excitement, and inspiration. Maintaining a connection to this place of emotional and spiritual potency is difficult amidst the overwhelming day-to-day responsibilities and hardships of teaching. As a leader I am well positioned and I must constantly develop strategies to help teachers remember, rekindle, and hold this fire as a source of strength, energy, and sustenance.

Teacher *and* Learner, Always

Just as teachers continue to learn from their students every day, leaders must also learn and grow as a result of their relationships with those they lead—students, staff, and families. Every community member has something to offer. By genuinely positioning myself as learner, I demonstrate to my community how deeply I value them, their wisdom, and their experience, while modeling the principle of lifelong growth.

"Close" to the Classroom

Ideally, the strongest teachers should be in the classroom among students. This, I believe, should also be true of those who are in positions of leadership. When it is not possible for leaders to continue to teach, they should remain as close to the classroom—and to the day-to-day experience of teachers and students—as possible. It is from this place of solidarity and sensitivity that they can best position themselves to work alongside their staff to move them forward and outward.

Duty and Solidarity

Being an educator is more than a job; with it comes a duty to our students, their families, and our communities. Leaders must model this sense of duty and stand alongside their teachers and staff in the struggle against systems of oppression. Through this relationship of mutual commitment grows a sense of solidarity and trust between leaders and school community.

Teaching is Political

Teaching takes place in a social and political context, which is not neutral nor objective. Myriad factors act on schools to shape their outcomes in service of the status quo. Developing one's craft and pedagogy involves reflecting critically on one's identity and making choices about where one stands in relationship to the institution of education in this country and the systems of oppression that are always impacting the lives of our students. The work of leadership must help teachers understand the political forces acting on schools and then navigate where they stand in the larger political and social context of education.

Put in the Work

Teachers work as hard as any other profession and do the most important work in the world. And the reality of teaching in urban education is that, no matter how strong or experienced one is, the work will never be easy. As a leader, I must stand shoulder to shoulder with my teachers and be willing to put in the work, even (especially) when it is difficult. I must exemplify the type of educators I expect my teachers and staff to be.

Using these Core Values as a cornerstone, Gardner was committed to remaining in tune with the experience of teachers, those who bore the greatest burden of educating our young people within a system that too often served more as a barrier than a support. He believed that if he had the right tools, if he worked as much and as hard as possible, and if he embodied passion for the work and the students, then his staff would stay inspired and the school would thrive.

And during his tenure at ARISE, in many ways it has thrived. By his second year at the school, he was starting to feel confident in his leadership—and the school, under a hard-working leadership team and deeply invested staff, was making progress.

Building on the foundation of an aspirational original vision and the excellent work of leaders and teachers who had come before, they had developed a school-wide coaching model to support every teacher; they had gained clarity on their instructional core and aligned that with their professional development map; their retention of teachers had improved; they were successfully modeling several elements of a discipline system rooted in restorative practices; and while they were philosophically opposed to standardized testing as the principal measure of success, students' scores had improved dramatically on standardized state tests.

Recognizing the importance of a positive staff culture, an element of leadership which, during his time in the classroom, he had not prioritized, Gardner even took the lead in writing a teacher retention grant that provided resources for teacher wellness activities and acknowledgments such as teacher of the month and what ARISE called teacher "Rising Suns," including the integration of a process of "adult reflection," a structure that provided the space and time for teachers to check in and discuss anything that was going on in their lives, inside or outside of school.

There was still so much room for growth, but the school was moving in a positive direction. Gardner believed his team was making many of the right moves—attending to both the technical and relational aspects of leadership as outlined by Margaret Wheatley and Tim Dalmau's "6-Circle Model" (1983), a framework that guides leaders to focus not only on process but also on how we make meaning and relate to one another in the work.

But he came to realize there was more to the puzzle of leadership than the technical and the relational. Instructional core rubrics, backward-mapped professional development plans, intentional conversations about identity, and a whole-school coaching model were important elements of a highly functional school, but they would soon come to realize that there was a deeper layer of work that needed more attention.

In the middle of the spring semester, teachers and staff began meeting and organizing, in private, to voice their concerns about overwhelming working conditions. Although they emphasized that the push back was about systems and structures and not directly about school leaders, Gardner was still stunned and saddened.

Leadership in schools can be demoralizing because, no matter what decisions leaders make or actions they take, it will rarely ever satisfy everyone. Leaders are pulled in multiple directions by the various stakeholders who expect them to take on the full weight of the burdens placed on schools.

In the same way, schools are expected to "fix" so many of society's injustices, those working within schools sometimes have a parallel expectation of leaders to "fix" all of the challenges within education. Balancing adequate personal responsibility while not taking the pressures and criticism personally is a relentless conundrum of school leadership.

Gardner had tried to embody his Core Values and had done everything he thought possible to support and nurture teachers, going out of his way to position himself as a servant leader and a strong teacher advocate. Still, it was not enough.

US AND THEM

His leadership team learned this lesson again at another point in the year when a serious incident with a student making social media threats to cause violence to his school community triggered explosive divisions within his staff. In response to the student's threats and the perception that it was not handled appropriately, a small group of teachers organized and pushed back against the administration and various other members of the school community. They believed the response to the threats, which included naming a few teachers as potential targets, was not as urgent as the situation merited.

Several other staff members reacted with judgment and condemnation of these teachers, and for the remainder of the school year, much of the time and energy of the school leadership was spent trying to hold boundaries of professionalism, put out fires that were ignited by staff members who were continually looking for excuses to blame and shame others, and rebuild broken relationships.

Staff had become disconnected not only from each other but from the belief in the collective purpose that kept them rooted in the same ground and, therefore, the belief that others around them were doing the best they could with what they had. In its place, dynamics of separation emerged, with some teachers presuming they were more dedicated, harder working, or more "down" than their colleagues.

The leadership team, feeling their own vulnerability and uncertainty about their handling of a situation for which there was no right answer, became ungrounded and responded with defensiveness, forgetting the foundation of community and purpose they had worked hard to construct. Gardner felt help-less as a leader and disconnected from the Core Values that were supposed to be his anchor.

Although the threats of violence to the school were the catalyst for this toxic adult culture, the underlying reasons were more deeply rooted in systems of oppression working beyond the view of these well-intentioned educators and the corresponding conditions they created. Their focus turned to looking for someone to hold accountable for the trauma they had experienced.

"Us and them" thinking is prevalent in schools and it is the source of much of the dysfunction experienced among staff. This plays out in many forms: teachers versus administration, "these" teachers versus "those" teachers, school staff blaming families or students, or even school leaders versus other school leaders.

Gardner passed through a series of reactions to the anger and dissatisfaction of the teachers and staff at ARISE: feeling exhausted and demoralized, like he had nothing left to give; fear that it meant the school was falling apart; anger at their lack of appreciation of his efforts; condemnation of their unwillingness to do what it takes to serve our students; blaming other leaders at his school; and uncertainty about his own leadership. He gave strong consideration to moving back into the classroom and teaching full time. He assessed whether or not he could disinvest and go simply through the motions of being an administrator. He even came close to leaving his school altogether.

But, here again he reflected on his Core Values to reorient himself, a process that was equal parts spiritual, emotional, and intellectual. Why did he do this work? What had kept him committed and inspired for the past twenty years? "Duty and Solidarity" kept emerging for him, like a heavy heartbeat during an arduous workout. His students, despite the turmoil, were showing up every day ready to learn. Families continued to invest their trust in the school. Parents even organized to increase their presence on campus in order to increase the sense of safety felt by all.

His decision was clear; he would stay put and commit even more deeply to leading his school toward becoming a truly transformative space for the students and families who had entrusted him and his staff with their education.

Gardner had two critical realizations during this tumultuous time. First, he understood that nothing was wrong or unreasonable about the teachers' expression of being overwhelmed and wanting their working conditions to be sustainable. The issues they raised were genuine and real; some of the most dedicated, brilliant, passionate teachers with whom he worked were feeling exhausted, stressed, and overwhelmed by work that never went away and educational needs that, in reality, would be left unmet if not for their unrelenting energy and support for their students.

Second, Gardner realized that the criticism and pushback were not aimed at him personally but, rather, about his leadership. Certainly, it would be an easy response to point to all the conditions that made success feel out of reach—the twelve-hour days with still more work to do, the average reading level his students at least two years behind grade level, the fact that Oakland has one of the lowest base salaries for teachers in the Bay Area—and these are all valid aspects of the beast.

Still, if he wanted to create the conditions for transformation at his school; if he wanted to change the system from within, he needed to become a more transformative leader.

COMMUNITY, SOLIDARITY, AND PURPOSE

As a teacher whose identity and life experiences were always different from those of the communities he served, Gardner understood "Teacher *and* Learner Always" as a necessary value in terms of his ability to authentically serve his students. This core value has guided the development a few fundamental elements of transformative leadership he has come to believe in.

Through reflection, study, dialogue, and struggle—a praxis that intensified in the wake of his leadership challenges but that has defined his life as an educator—three that he has found to be paramount are:

1. Community: Take care of one another and stay grounded in the mission
2. Solidarity: Build critical consciousness toward collective action
3. Purpose: Fuel the fire

COMMUNITY: TAKE CARE OF ONE ANOTHER AND STAY GROUNDED IN THE MISSION

In August, two weeks before the beginning of every school year, Gardner gathers his entire staff at his childhood home in Ukiah, two hours north of the school in Oakland. This has been a practice at the past three schools where he has taught and led and has been a tradition at ARISE since he started there five years ago. His entire staff (it is mandatory paid professional development) spends two days together cooking, swimming, playing goofy community building games, sharing stories of their paths into education, and staying up late into the night.

There is an agenda for the two days and they do work to prepare for the year, including meeting in departments and grade level teams to set goals and review the academic targets for the year, but the true value of the preschool-year retreat comes through in the moments outside of the agenda, where relationships are established, deepened, and sometimes repaired, and where staff members take time to genuinely *see* one another.

Significant time is invested in the retreat; with only about eight total days of professional development before the first day of school, 25 percent of their time together as a staff is dedicated almost solely to community building. But the community that begins to establish itself during the retreat provided a foundation and a touch point for the rest of the year, one that is essential, most importantly during family conference week, Warrior Intellectual Portfolio Defense presentations, or the late-October stretch—those highly taxing times of the year when everyone in the building is running on fumes and staff are most prone to turning toward others for responsibility and blame.

In building connections among staff, it is critical to remember that communities are unique and that one's school community is rooted in the students and families it serves with a particular mission and vision. The mission of ARISE High School is to:

BOX 2.2

Empower ourselves with the skills, knowledge, and agency to become highly educated, humanizing, critically conscious, intellectual, and reflective leaders in our community.

At ARISE we nurture, train, and discipline our school community to engage in a continuous practice of developing mind, heart, and body toward a VISION where we actively rise up. Agency and self-determination drive our struggle to improve our own material and social conditions toward a more healthy, equitable, and just society.

All of the work we do in our schools, including community building, should be in service of our mission. But what is also true is that, even though the mission stands as the enduring foundation, each year is unique, each combination of students and staff, each chemistry of interactions is different. Leaders must be highly attuned to these dynamics and improvise each year.

Therefore, it is necessary to design activities that ask our staff to explicitly make meaning of and build a relationship to the mission, both individually and collectively. This work also starts during our retreat. Each year the activities are refined but we generally lead staff in a personal reflection on the mission, followed by a public sharing, then a collective visioning of how we plan to make the mission live in our classrooms, our school, and our community.

One such mission-centering activity involved one of our veteran teachers leading every staff member in turning our wordy mission and vision statement into a six-word statement that they believed best captured the essence of what ARISE was about. We then read them all aloud, narrowed them down to the favorite selections, and voted on the one that staff most felt embodied our mission and vision. That six-word statement (actually, the one we chose was only five words: "Empowering Critically Conscious Warrior Intellectuals") was then placed onto t-shirts and sweatshirts that we printed for everyone to wear.

Another year, our mission-centering activity integrated our school's focus on restorative justice circles as a central pedagogical strategy. Toward the end of our retreat, we asked all staff members to reflect on their own interpretation of the mission and a unique way they imagined making it live in the work they do with young people at ARISE.

We then gathered in a large circle with a ball of yarn that was tossed from one educator to another as each shared out their commitment to living the mission. In the end, we had created a physical web that connected every member of the staff to each other through our commitments to the ARISE mission and our students.

The power in these examples lies both in the experience of making collective meaning around the mission that brings us together as a school community as well as the symbolic centerpiece to which we can return throughout the year to remind us of why we do the work that we do.

But the community building at the retreat is just the first stitch in a cloth we weave throughout the year with the intention of continually deepening, broadening, and repairing our connections as a staff. An important element of this cloth that we repeat every week is an appreciation process that we call "much loves." At the end of each staff meeting, we close the space by offering "much love" to any colleague or community member whom we wish to recognize for going out of their way to contribute to our individual or collective success that week.

These appreciations range from recognizing a teacher who stepped in to cover a class when another teacher was out sick to a much love for a staff member who made the time to check in with another who was having a difficult day. Although the practice takes only a few minutes every week, it creates a powerful space to tend to the heart in the midst of work that is so often focused only on the head.

One of the Core Values that Gardner identified as central to his leadership is the balance between "Urgency and Patience." Adapted from his reading of Paulo Freire's *Teachers as Cultural Workers*, these principles can be perceived as, and often exist as competing energies when it comes to work in schools. However, one critical mistake school leaders, especially new leaders, make is to err too much on the side of urgency when it comes to their staff. We tend to rationalize: they are adults and can take care of themselves, they just need to do their jobs, or they should have known what they were getting into when they became an educator.

And, while all of these refrains may be true, strong leadership involves the patience to have empathy and compassion for the relentless nature of teaching and to create school environments in which all community members feel a sense of care and dignity in their work. The urgency will follow.

SOLIDARITY: BUILD CRITICAL CONSCIOUSNESS TOWARD COLLECTIVE ACTION

The nature of the beast is to place educators under conditions where it is impossible to be successful at all the things they are responsible for doing with and for their students. It eats them up. They look for blame. Why is this work so hard? Why is it constantly overwhelming? The beast is effective because it is so pervasive that it can be invisible.

One of the fundamental challenges of school leadership is getting the educators in a school to identify and understand the beast and to build a sense of solidarity in the face of what Baldwin aptly names, "the most fantastic, the most brutal, and the most determined resistance."

Moving from "us and them" thinking to the understanding that we are all connected in the work requires a sincere reflection on the part of staff and a critical analysis of the position of schools in society—the same development of critical consciousness that we work to engage in with our students.

No one chooses to be an educator in a historically marginalized and under-resourced community like East Oakland and myriad other communities around the world because the work is easy, because they intend to harm or neglect young people, or because it is a simple way to earn a paycheck. People overwhelmingly get into this work out of a sense of purpose and a desire to impact positively the communities in which they work.

One of the most common reasons given for entering the teaching profession is a commitment to social justice and a belief that teaching is the most impactful way to create a more just world. Consequently, school leaders should operate under two assumptions (even if they are not true in every case): (1) Everyone is doing the best they can with what they have at any given moment, and (2) factors beyond their control—Baldwin's "determined resistance"—exert a powerful influence over their ability to achieve transformative outcomes for their students.

In order to build a culture grounded in these precepts, in the context of a work environment that already asks much more of educators than is possible to achieve, leaders must shape an inclusive culture of solidarity upon which schools organize a resistance to the status quo in service of the liberation of their students. While different staff members may not agree on the exact methods of achieving this goal, there must be solidarity—"unity or agreement of feeling or action, especially among individuals with a common interest"—in the goal of giving the best possible education to all students as in alignment with the mission of the school.

At ARISE High School, this means empowering students to "rise up" and working to "improve our own social and material conditions towards a more healthy, equitable, and just society."

To achieve cohesion, it is incumbent upon school leaders to build trust and extinguish the divisions that emerge so easily among people working together under such overwhelming conditions.

One key step is to engage one's school community in the critical consciousness building that helps them identify the nature of the resistance they face.

Leaders must engage their staffs in both window and mirror thinking. They must look out the window at the social, political, economic, and cultural barriers standing in the way of their students. Instead of ignoring these systems of oppression and simply expecting students and educators to work harder, persevere, and cultivate grit, leaders must engage directly with the food deserts, gang violence, mass incarceration and police brutality, attacks on immigrants, and unemployment that spin a web of trauma in the lives of so many of our young people.

They need to hold space for the frustration, anger, and righteous indignation that arise and move this energy toward collective action. A staff taking collective action against the true forces of opposition to our students' livelihoods and education, an adversary beyond the walls of our classrooms and schools, is less likely to turn toward each other for blame when the conditions of their work become unbearable.

As a school leader, the decision to advocate, organize, or even create the space for collective action can be precarious and intimidating given the complex political nature of the work and the inevitable pushback that will come from those who oppose the decision or the action, dissent that might include one's own boss, the district, and even some parents and community. But courageous leadership in support of collective action against forces that oppress our community is one of the most powerful ways to build solidarity among one's teachers and staff.

This collective action has taken myriad forms throughout the years at ARISE as it is a foundational element at our school. Gardner recalls the decision of his leadership team to publicly declare their school a sanctuary school in the wake of newly elected president Trump's anti-immigrant wave in 2017.

Though this decision was neither morally bold nor unique, especially for a school in the Bay Area, the actions that followed—sending letters home to parents, providing professional development time to discuss what it meant to be a solidarity school, putting up signage around the school, and supporting students and staff in walkouts and marches to protest dehumanizing immigration policies—put the school at some potential risk.

As with the commitment to community building, it is challenging to find time for the work of building critical consciousness, but the time spent reacting to divisions and conflict with adult culture will be far more consuming in the long run if this work is not done preemptively.

This is inherently political work (as Gardner's 6th Core Value asserts)—and political work in schools is tricky and fraught with risk. In their seminal work on the history of schooling in the United States, *Schooling in Capitalist America*, Bowles and Gintiss shine a light on the hidden curriculum in schools and the way that schools in this country have always served the status quo:

> The educational system does not add to or subtract from the overall degree of inequality and repressive personal development. Rather, it is best understood as an institution which serves to perpetuate the social relationships of economic life through which these patterns are set, by facilitating a smooth integration of youth into the labor force. (Bowles and Gintiss 2012, 11)

Unfortunately, this text and others like it, such as bell hooks's *Teaching to Transgress,* Jay Gillen's *Educating for Insurgency,* and the various works of Paulo Freire are not prevalent in the curriculum of most teacher development programs.

Most educators, believing in the virtue and importance of their occupation, begin their careers with minimal critical analysis of the institution in which they will be working. Then, once their tenure begins, they are so overwhelmed and busy that developing a critical analysis of schooling is low on their list of priorities. Unless they teach in an already radicalized school or region, or make a connection to radical educator organizations such as the Bay Area's Teachers 4 Social Justice or New York Collective of Radical Educators, then a political education that problematizes the role of schools in society is probably far from their focus.

Transformative school leaders must find ways to build into their work a curriculum that raises the critical consciousness of their entire staff in order to build a sense of solidarity in the face of very real and present oppressive forces.

While there are no shortcuts or silver bullets here, and there is no way to develop solidarity and critical consciousness among one's staff without dedicating significant time and energy to the endeavor, there are ways to incorporate this work in a way that feels integrated and complementary instead of it being perceived as another responsibility adding to already-full plates.

Differentiated reading groups is one powerful means of developing critical consciousness with staff in a way that recognizes that, just as with our technical skills in the classroom, educators come to schools with widely divergent beliefs, ideologies, experiences, and awareness when it comes to the realities of our students and communities. Leaders should assess (and have their staff self-assess) their strengths and areas of growth in terms of critical consciousness, then design reading groups based on this assessment.

Reading groups can function in multiple ways. The key is to focus on themes that help advance the awareness and thinking of participants in relation to the students and communities they serve while engaging in the process of making meaning together through study, reflection, and dialogue.

At a given time, a school might have one group of educators focused on the dynamics of being white and teaching mostly students of color and reading Robin DiAngelo's *White Fragility* or Lisa Delpit's *Other People's Children*, another group examining the school-to-prison pipeline and the alternative practices of restorative justice, and still another group looking at the complexities of identity that many of our students navigate through Gloria Anzaldua's *Borderlands/La Frontera*.

Another excellent way to build solidarity around critical consciousness is through collaborative projects connected to social justice. Teachers working together on projects that engage their students in their own critical consciousness development and while having a direct impact on their communities is not only a strong pedagogical strategy but doubly beneficial as it pushes the thinking of both students and staff.

At ARISE High School, the tenth grade team developed a project entitled "Machismo Mata, Mata Machismo" (there is not a direct translation for the Spanish work "machismo" but the most accurate translation is something like "Male Chauvinism Kills, Kill Male Chauvinism") which focused on the essential question, How does patriarchy and machismo impact health in our community? Teachers in Geometry, World Cultures, English, Spanish, and Biology classes collaborated on various aspects of the project, which culminated in students presenting their research and recommendations to sixth and seventh graders at local middle schools.

Home visits are another method of developing critical consciousness by stepping into the lives of the young people we serve in order to more deeply understand them and what it means to serve them in our schools.

While these practices represent a few concrete ways that school leaders can build solidarity and critical consciousness, we must be mindful not to overwhelm our staff with a sense that the beast is too powerful to overcome.

We must give name and form to the forces acting against our young people but not allow them to become an excuse for failure, an external enemy that paralyzes us in the belief that the power of the status quo is too immense to overcome. The risk of looking out the window at all of the factors beyond our control is that it provides a potential justification for inaction. In order to balance out the weight of these forces, leaders need to engender a sense of responsibility and find ways to fuel the fire of hope and possibility.

PURPOSE: FUEL THE FIRE

Fueling the fire is about focusing on the heart in the midst of work that is so often about thinking and doing. What is your why? What brought you to the work of education? What has kept you going for three, seven, twelve, twenty-three years? This is the most important question leaders can ask their teachers and staff—one that they must come back to continually in order to maintain a sense of hope and possibility during the most challenging times and an energy of inspiration and creativity throughout the year.

There is no way educators can sustain their work in schools that serve historically marginalized and under-resourced communities without a sense of purpose and a passion for what they do. But this energy can be quickly extinguished beneath the weight of the overwhelming conditions described in this chapter. Too often, urban schools' resources, especially human resources, are stretched so thinly that educators become disconnected from their whys.

Leaders can prevent this, to some extent, by creating space for their staffs to share their stories of what brought them to education in the first place. The sharing is a ceremonial space where every story is listened to and respected, regardless of the nature of the story or the place a given individual may be in along their educational journey.

Although staff members inevitably have vastly different experiences and realities, some of which mirror many of the backgrounds of our students and others that could not be more different, the opportunity is to connect around the heart of the work by understanding the motivations and decisions that brought each member of the community to the work of education.

Fueling the fire also requires leaders to know and understand what inspires each member of their staff, what is the source of their passion and excitement in the work. This is different for everyone, so a commitment to building relationships is key. Shane Safir offers a treasure trove of ideas and practices for the relational work of leadership in her valuable book *The Listening Leader*, the primary principle being the connection between a leader's ability to generate trust and connection with staff and the potential for transformational and equitable outcomes for students (Safir 2017).

To take it a step further, and drawing on Zaretta Hammond's concept of learning partnerships, investing in relationship development that goes beyond simply mutual respect but that earns teachers the right to demand engagement and effort, leaders must invest in their teachers and staff members in such a way that they earn the right to push them beyond what they believe they are capable of (Hammond 2015).

Getting outside of the classroom and the school building can be a potent way to fuel, or re-fuel the fire and even to connect educators to a greater sense of purpose. Since his first year of teaching, Gardner has organized and led camping, backpacking, and international travel trips with his students.

These trips have always served as opportunities for him to connect, learn, and deepen relationships beyond the classroom walls, rare opportunities for educators and students to authentically humanize each other as individual beings not confined to the roles assigned to them by their positions within the institution of school. However, as he grew into leadership, Gardner realized that one of the most powerful aspects of these trips was the way they inspired the other educators who came along on the trips and both rejuvenated and deepened their sense of purpose in the work.

Now, as a school leader, he uses camping trips that he leads about five times per year for students as a tool for intentionally engaging staff members, sometimes those who seem disconnected or uninspired, those who are struggling to build connections with challenging students, or those whose fire he wants to spread to other staff members who need revitalization.

Finally, fire requires oxygen—and that oxygen for educators comes in the form of the time and energy to do what they love and what they are passionate about in service of their students. We have already established that the nature of the beast is to maintain conditions that make the work overwhelming and unsustainable. Still, leaders must dream beyond these constraints and continually find creative ways to fill their schools with oxygen.

At ARISE, most recently, leaders have invested in teacher sustainability interviews with every teacher in the school to interrogate what changes, within our realm of control, leaders could promote to make the work more sustainable and make them want to stay for longer tenures (see Box 2.3 for a list of teacher sustainability interview questions). The feedback from these interviews is being used to make systemic shifts in teaching assignments, schedules, and school initiatives.

BOX 2.3 TEACHER SUSTAINABILITY INTERVIEW QUESTIONS

- Why did you choose to teach at ARISE?
- What inspires you to work here?
- How long do you see yourself ideally teaching at ARISE? What factors influence this?
- What are the most challenging aspects of working at ARISE that are within our control?

- Our model is very complex and has many different moving parts beyond classroom teaching. If you could eliminate two to three of those moving parts, what would they be and why?
- If you could choose between a significant raise or an additional non-teaching period next year, which would you choose and why?
- What other potential changes that are within our control would make teaching at ARISE more sustainable and make you want to work here for the long run?

In chapter 4, Meredith Gavrin offers a thorough explanation of how she works hard to protect her teachers' ability to think critically, be creative, and take risks in their classrooms, another important way a leader can help produce oxygen to fuel the fires.

CONCLUSION

According to a recent study by the School Leaders Network, 50 percent of new school principals quit during their third year in the position, and less than 30 percent stay beyond year five. Given this data, we must conclude one of two things, either people who go into school leadership are quitters who have little investment in their work and their schools, or that the appropriate systems and structures necessary to support the success of these leaders are not in place in most schools and districts.

Having taught and led in multiple different schools throughout the Bay Area for over twenty years, and having consulted with hundreds of teacher and school leaders throughout the nation, Gardner has concluded that the rate of turnover is not a result of the lack of desire, commitment, or willingness to put in the work on the part of leaders.

The problem is systemic; and, as argued throughout this chapter and this book, it is intentional and predictable. We must fight collectively for systemic change.

However, in the meantime, until we change the system of education so that it truly works to create fair and equitable outcomes for all children, especially those who come from historically marginalized and under-resourced communities, leaders must find ways to work within the institution to create conditions for transformation and liberation. We owe it to our students, who have no alternative but the schools that we currently provide them, to be the best possible leaders imaginable. Even if the building is falling apart, we cannot simply leave it. After all, the children are still inside.

REFLECTIVE QUESTIONS FOR LEADING
IN THE BELLY OF THE BEAST

1. Why did you get into teaching and education? What was your purpose in becoming a school leader? How do you continually communicate this purpose to your staff and your school community?
2. When and how are you building in opportunities for your staff to communicate their whys to each other?
3. What keeps you grounded and focused on your purpose when challenges and conflicts arise? What routines and practices have you developed to remain clear about your purpose and vision?
4. How do you define community? Do your teachers and staff genuinely care about each other? What routines and practices do you use to *authentically* build and maintain community at your school?
5. How are students involved in community building at your school?
6. What are the most prevalent systems and forces acting to oppress your students and community every day? How are you supporting your staff to learn about and develop critical consciousness around these forces?
7. In what ways do you center the voices of the teachers and staff most impacted by the same systems and forces of oppression experienced by your students?
8. What is your role in supporting your teachers and staff in taking collective action beyond your school? What do you need to do to show up as an ally for them?

NOTES

1. *In the context of this chapter, I am using the term educators to describe anyone working directly with and, therefore, in relationship with, students in a school setting. This ranges from administrators and teachers to parent coordinators, counselors, school therapists, and secretaries.*
2. For a more in-depth reflection on how Gardner's identity influences his leadership, see his chapter "There is No Such Thing as Woke" in a forthcoming book also published by Rowman and Littlefield.

Chapter 3

Leading with "Tenacious Love"
Kristin Botello

Seek, too, a leader who aspires to a noble ideal of education. Noble because the work of transforming children's lives is particularly ennobling. Noble because the work has merit only when done for no reason except to transform children's lives. Noble because the work is necessary work in the highest sense of mission—what one is sent to do for others . . . And once you've identified the leader who will spearhead your new creation, surround him or her with a group of insanely dedicated followers, a few people who can infect the rest of the staff with the values and ideals that make education or any work exciting, fruitful, and worthwhile.

—Lorraine Monroe

INTRODUCTION

The *belly of the beast* thrives in South Los Angeles. Here the beast feeds on the self-fulfilling prophecy of black and brown men, who cannot imagine a life past the age of twenty. The beast lives through young women who believe predatory men, when they proclaim love only to gain access to their bodies.

The beast lives in the streets and in the street dwellers, in the danger, the trash, the drugs, and the gangs. The beast is the neglect of an entire sector of the city, and in turn the neglect of an entire group of people, deemed dispensable due to their race, economic status, or ethnicity. It makes it almost impossible to succeed here. So, how can a small high school of 600 students exist, creating a tiny oasis of hope for thirteen years, right in the middle of the belly?

Animo Jackie Robinson Charter High School is located in Los Angeles, thirty blocks south of downtown Los Angeles, and just east of the University of Southern California. In fact, a young person can take a five-minute walk from AJR to USC under the 110 freeway bridge and experience two vastly distinct worlds. On the west end, exists a swiftly moving society of power and privilege in the midst of newly built, pristine buildings, shops, eateries, and bicyclists with smiling college students working toward and achieving academic, personal, and financial success.

On the east end, humble, hard-working black and brown families navigate a maze of extreme poverty, desperation, and violence. Students are here, too, but these students focus primarily on surviving. Simultaneously, they are trying to distinguish a path that makes sense to *them*, a path they can see *themselves* traveling, a path that leads to a better life. They have seen and lived through challenges that most USC students could never imagine, and they, too, are striving for more, something unseen and unimagined.

In 2006, to alleviate the challenges of overcrowding and under-serving masses of students in the public high schools in South Los Angeles, Green Dot Public School founder, Steve Barr, encouraged Dr. Lori Pawinski and Kristin Botello to open up Animo Jackie Robinson Charter High School (AJR) in this area. They opened their doors to 140 ninth graders and their families and have since grown to serve 600 high school students each year on a co-located campus of William Clinton Middle School.

Their tiny high school exists among myriad small charter and pilot high schools in Los Angeles, which have experienced success across a spectrum of student performance measures. It is one among many choices for families looking for an alternative to the "factory model" high schools in the area. So what makes this school special?

AJR was built in an industrial sector of South Los Angeles that cannot be called a neighborhood. Factories border the school on all four sides, and students do not walk past any trees, homes, or lawns to get to school. There is no beauty on those streets. Rather, the streets are lined with homeless encampments and trash. Students take the bus or walk swiftly past store fronts and alleys, sometimes in groups, sometimes alone, looking straight and guarding themselves with hoods pulled tightly over their heads.

Families live in extreme poverty, and that poverty permeates every aspect of the students' lives. It is rare that a student's physical, economic circumstances in this sector of the city change. However, a young person *can* change her attitude and perspective about her agency here, she *can* shift her ability to better navigate her life's circumstances. When a student can be clear about what she wants, what she is willing to accept and what she must reject, then we have given her power to rewrite her story. This is the mission of Animo Jackie Robinson.

SYSTEMATIZING LOVE

Within the school community at AJR, the collective experience of transformation grows out of individual transformation, and individual transformation occurs because of a transformed self-concept. The school leader, Ms. Botello, believes that *self-love* is a force strong enough to overcome the erosive power of generational, complex trauma that pervades the inner cities. It is the metaphorical hill that she stands on and refuses to waiver from, despite the potential skepticism of any newcomer to the school.

Love is strong, not weak, she contends. It is a force that can propel folks of any age to do seemingly impossible things. It is obvious when love is lacking in a community, and it is also evident when love thrives there. It is almost palpable. At AJR, adults fuel their work with tenacious love and teach their students to love themselves and to use that self-love to flip the narrative of their lives and to disrupt the predictability of their outcomes, because at this school, in this family, students don't feel alone or unsupported. They feel safe enough to open up to the support that adults have to offer, and they are able to learn and grow and *change*.

ONE AT A TIME

Educators have a tendency to focus their work on creating systems and programs that they believe will transform the existing building as a whole, but Ms. Botello's philosophy of school transformation is that *intimacy* fosters real change. In successful schools, collective, sustained transformation happens one person at a time. Sustained change can only be real through the vehicle of personal relationships and that requires risk-taking on the part of both people.

It is the responsibility of the adults to take the first risk. It is the responsibility and the privilege of the leader in a school to model that risk-taking for the other adults. The magic happens when students are convinced that your moves to know them are authentic and they let you in. But how can a school leader or any educator authentically reach out to young people, particularly students of color, who have been historically marginalized by school?

Students are keen observers of human dynamics. They know what they know, and you cannot fool them. They know when you want to know them, and they know when you don't need or desire to connect. Educators can talk the talk of empathy, building positive relationships and making connections, but the truth is, the hurt that students living in poverty experience *on the daily* makes them wise judges of character.

They are critical thinkers who can analyze intention. They can see truth; they can smell it. They understand shams, posturing, and sympathy. They recognize pity; and superficial attempts to "relate" mean nothing to them. In fact, these attempts are disrespectful. True relationships, which are necessary to promote much-needed change in the lives and attitudes of young people in low-income neighborhoods, grow out of honesty, a real desire to get to know them, one at a time.

A LEADER'S CLARITY OF PURPOSE

Without the singular vision of a dedicated leader and without commitment to that vision, a small school can simply exist, recycling strategies, programs, and systems that schools in all shapes and sizes have implemented in the past with little success. Not much will change if the leader and the leader's team are not clear about their purpose—so clear that they build all the components of the school, based on meeting that goal.

For a transformational leader like Ms. Botello, that purpose is simple, yet extremely difficult to achieve—a school leader must shift the self-concept of her students and develop agency in them to rewrite their own personal narratives, through tenacious love. It is truly believing that each student can achieve this goal and convince the other adults and, most importantly, the students themselves, that they *can* be better and make themselves smarter without changing who they are at the core.

GROW OTHERS IN ORDER TO FULFILL AND SUSTAIN THE MISSION: YOU CANNOT DO IT ALONE

Most adults go into teaching to do just that—teach. They are trained to teach algebra, physics, English, or history, not to deal with difficult psychological or social emotional situations with young people. But in schools situated in communities of poverty, all the adults in the building are asked to take on a significant amount of additional responsibility in mentoring and guiding students as they navigate their lives. The most successful teachers are able to develop meaningful, positive relationships with their students, who can offer support in a plethora of ways to the young people with whom they interact.

However, adults in schools like AJR are often overwhelmed as well. They are unable to give when they are not receiving and being nourished, both professionally and personally. Ms. Botello recognizes the very real need of the adults who also must be fortified regularly in an authentic way in order to weather the relentless storm of ghetto life. In *Culturally Responsive Teaching and the Brain*, Zaretta Hammond discusses validation and affirmation as authentic ways to build rapport in relationships with students (Hammond 2014). Ms. Botello and the school leaders intentionally affirm and validate students in their daily work and also infuse affirmation and validation into their professional development approaches to teachers and other adults.

Ms. Botello listens to her staff, even when she disagrees with them, and validates their voices when making whole-school decisions. This approach to teacher development may seem obvious and even basic—listen to folks and incorporate their voice into your decision-making and leadership. It is, however, disturbingly lacking in many urban schools, where teachers and staff often feel as powerless and stuck as the students do.

Ms. Botello's goal is to grow and nurture administrators and teachers in the same way she commits to growing students, by establishing a safe space for discourse and risk-taking and by fostering their self-confidence and self-love. This approach helps to ensure that she maintains a strong team of educators who want to stay at her school and implement the collective vision because they genuinely feel supported and encouraged. The work is a marathon rather than a sprint. Transformation is gradual, and a team of educators need to remain committed to each other and their collective goal in order to help students achieve that transformation.

Sometimes Ms. Botello's unwavering commitment to the gradual transformation of students leaves teachers impatient. They seek faster change in students who struggle both academically and behaviorally. They work with these young people every day and are tired; sometimes the struggle feels too great, so much so that it is demoralizing. Sometimes Botello must stand firm behind the purpose she established years ago, through her twenty years of classroom experience and teacher leadership with students of color in impoverished communities.

She must ask her people to have faith in the long haul. It is challenging and often there is a need for courageous conversations, but somehow the adults trust the culture of the school community and trust Botello to help them ride out the difficulties. The "ride-or-die's" remain steadfast, and for Botello so far, it has worked to be more tenacious with love for students (and the adults who work with them) than the forces that seek to overwhelm them. She is unwavering in her support for students first, but also for teachers first. This is the paradox that works for Botello.

Both the students and the adults who work with them need to be affirmed and validated and honored for their work and their life experiences, even when they make mistakes. Everyone is growing and everyone needs a chance. People who hurt others are also people who are hurting, so she urges them to take a moment to walk in one another's shoes.

At Animo Jackie Robinson, Botello is committed to equity, even when it's hard. Every person receives what they need, and that includes adults and students. Sometimes this doesn't feel "fair," because it isn't equal, but it is what is necessary for everyone to thrive. Botello understands that she must be empathetic with her staff and her students and she must teach them to have empathy as well, *but for real, though*, not because empathy is a buzzword or a current fad. Leaders must be real and model forgiveness, but not blind forgiveness—forgiveness coupled with modeling and high expectations.

Leaders need to show staff members in the building *how* to be vulnerable, own their mistakes, and model learning from those mistakes in order to teach students to be better themselves. It takes time and commitment and the leader cannot do it alone.

The concept of "systematizing love" can seem abstract and difficult to conceptualize or operationalize for school leaders who may be reading this book. How does a leader make love actionable within the system and structure of a public school? This sounds too corny, too cheesy to be real, right? It seems that the power of societal stressors, combined with the pressures of academic accountability for student performance are too strong, too rigid, too overwhelming. Ms. Botello shares stories that represent dozens of examples of how a leader can systematize love for students and adults in a learning community. Each story illustrates eight core components of Ms. Botello's theory of transformation at her school.

- Replicate the commitment
- Honor real work
- Little things in a big way
- Confront with love
- Facilitate greatness
- Create a safe space through vulnerability and honesty
- Everything matters—consistent care
- Protect folks

RYAN, JASMIN, AND OSCAR:
REPLICATE THE COMMITMENT

Through the years at AJR various students have experienced unthinkable loss and tragedies that have the potential to destroy young people, or at the very least, derail them in their quest for success in *college, leadership, and life* (the mission of Green Dot Public Schools, the CMO that includes Animo Jackie Robinson, is to transform public education in order to help all students prepare for college, leadership, and life). Most of these traumatic events are unpredictable and many of them are life changing. Students in urban areas need adults who are willing to reach into themselves to provide an unending well of support for them to be able to withstand these events. Ryan and Jasmin were able to do this for their student, Oscar.

Oscar had always been one of the top students in his class. He was the senior class president and in the running for class valedictor Roy. He was super creative, an artist and videographer. He was always a positive spirit, and he cared for others and led the students with Angel and enthusiasm. He was an athlete, playing for the football and men's volleyball teams. Everyone loved Oscar. He was also undocumented and needed a scholarship if he were to be able to attend college.

Ms. Botello and his teachers all hoped he would earn the scholarship he needed, and he got it—the blue and gold scholarship to UC Berkeley. He was going to attend the school of his dreams! He had made it! Due to his significantly low income and his undocumented status, he would need help, even for registration and transportation. Dr. Ryan McDonnell, the assistant principal, and Ms. Jasmin Gonzalez, his advisory teacher, would come through for him. They and others would put up the funds he needed to fulfill his dream, because they knew he deserved the help.

During the summer before his freshman year in college, Ms. Gonzalez called Ms. Botello at home. She was distraught and in tears.

"You won't believe it if I told you."

"Tell me," Ms. Botello responded. "Just say it."

"Oscar's dad died." She let out with a sigh. "He took his own life." She continued, "And Oscar is away at Summer Bridge at Cal." Ms. Botello and Ms. G. cried together on the phone. They did not speak for long, because they already knew what they must do.

"How will we get him home?"

"I'm going to call Ryan. We'll drive up and get him." Both women knew immediately that Oscar could not fly and that he had no one and no money to get home to his family. They knew he wouldn't ask for help. They also knew they would take care of it, and they knew Ryan would be there for Oscar as well. Jasmin called her student. She comforted him and discussed his plan. He decided that he would stay at Cal and complete Summer Bridge. He wouldn't waste his scholarship, and he would still attend in the Fall as planned.

His mother explained that they had all sacrificed too much for him to stop now, before he even had a chance to begin. His father would have wanted him to continue to pursue his goals. Oscar would just need to be home for a few days to support his mother and sister as they bore the weight of immediate grief and shock, and to prepare the funeral services. The two adults traveled six hours each way to pick up their student and bring him home to his mother. He stayed home for a week and then returned to school.

Two years later, Oscar and his family are still recovering from their loss. Oscar is still at Cal, and despite the fact that he was a second language learner, despite the fact that the expectations at UC Berkeley are tremendously high and he has struggled, he has been able to succeed and even thrive.

He has become a leader of other students of color at Cal. He was and continues to be stronger than he knew he could be. He serves as a role model for students who continue to visit Cal, choose to attend there, and seek the advice of those who have come before them. He is there because the adults at his school helped him leverage his own resilience and helped him reach deep into himself to muster the courage to persevere, even against the most overwhelming odds. He has gained the skills he needs to succeed at the university level, but the resilience? He had it all along, and his teachers and mentors won't let him forget this fact.

MAVIS: HONOR REAL WORK

It takes a special individual to do the work of transforming the lives of young people through the vehicle of education, especially in the poorest neighborhoods in our country, in our time. In the late 1990s, Dr. Lorraine Monroe, the founder of the Frederick Douglass Academy in New York City, spoke at a leadership conference that Ms. Botello attended. She was speaking about school transformation in the inner city. To an audience of about 300 school reformers, this tiny woman stared at them, wagged her finger in scolding manner and stated,

> All you people here are *crazy*! That's right, I said you're all crazy! It takes a crazy person to do the work of educating the students who most of the world views as dispensable, invisible children . . . . It takes a crazy person to do the work that never seems to get easier, despite our best efforts, because poverty and trauma continue to strike at our children and their families, like waves in the ocean . . . so thank God for the crazies.

Ms. Botello never forgot the words of Dr. Monroe, and when she founded her own school in 2006, she realized that a major part of her job was to make sure she hired folks who were as "crazy" and committed to do the real work as she was. Mavis Tevaga (pronounced *Tevonga*) was one of those crazies.

Ms. Tevaga has never and will never trivialize the work of advocating for her students, while simultaneously being the teacher who is hardest on them and pushes them the most. As the students say, "Ms. Tevaga don't play!" She is the chair of the Special Education department at AJR and has been a special educator there for the last eleven years.

Over the years, she has wanted to leave the school only once, when the school was failing to equip the department with both the human and material resources they needed to truly serve the students. When Ms. Botello became principal in 2012, Ms. Tevaga hoped that things would improve, especially since Ms. Botello was the mother of an autistic son. The two women spoke to each other in a heart-to-heart conversation.

"Miss, I can't keep doing this without real help."

"I know, miss. What do you need?" Mavis had been preparing for this conversation. She knew all the things the school could do to better serve its growing population of students with special needs.

"We need to convince the teachers that don't really want to do the work to leave, and we need to hire more skilled, dedicated special educators. We need our teachers to agree to have hybrid schedules, which will include some Resource classes and some Special Day Classes. We need to teach the general education teachers how to effectively accommodate their lessons and assessments. You need to help me to provide the professional development that will make them better partners in education special needs students. We need to revamp our Academic Success support classes to better serve our students in smaller, more structured classroom settings. We need one more teacher and one more Instructional Aide. We need our own computer cart. We need our own classrooms." The list went on and on, but Ms. Botello made a commitment to Mavis then and there.

"I will get you what you need. We will make this better for all our SPED students."

Currently, AJR has about 100 students with special needs, which means they make up about one-sixth of the entire school population. Over a period of about five years, Ms. Botello came through on her promise to get the Special Education department what they needed, and they in turn have become one of the most successful departments in the school. In fact, AJR has built a reputation in the local middle schools and surrounding community through word of mouth. Parents know that if they have a child with special needs, they should send them to AJR.

"They will really teach them there and your baby will be safe—no bullying" is what parents say to each other. Parents recognize and value that the teachers of special education classes at AJR refuse to dumb-down their curriculum or baby their students. They set measurable goals, they push students and they push each other. They focus on teaching their students to be independent learners. They incorporate transition lessons into their Academic Success curriculum and they have their students prepare for and take the SAT.

In 2017, Mavis became certified in proctoring the accommodated SAT. In the graduating class of 2018, three special education students were accepted into the California State University system. The following year thirteen students were accepted in CSU schools. Mavis and her team effectively opened the doors to college for their students with IEPs, because they simply would not give up on them and would not lower their expectations for their performance.

All the seniors in special education are required to complete the same graduation requirements of every other senior. Teachers work to modify tasks and assessments, but every student completes the requirements. More importantly, though, the students with special needs at the school do not feel ashamed. They have nothing to hide, because by the end of their four years at AJR, they have learned to love and accept themselves for who they are. This is Mavis Tevaga's version of tenacious love.

LAMAR: LITTLE THINGS IN A BIG WAY

Educational reformers continuously work on creating systems and revising curricular and social programs and approaches to students of color in low-income communities. Educators are constantly searching for answers to seemingly unsolvable problems our students and their teachers are facing. Often, though, systems don't seem to get at the real issues or reach the real students. On the ground floor, in school buildings and classrooms, the story is the same. Students arrive at school guarded and humble at the same time. They are hard *and* soft. They wear masks for protection, and they desperately want someone to help them discard them. They are distant, yet they seek closeness. They camouflage themselves with hoodies that encapsulate their insecurities and shade their fears. They are smart, knowledgeable, even cynical, and yet they want to learn and know more. They are skeptics about love and hope, who want to be proven wrong. They avoid adults, and yet they want someone to reach out, reach in, connect to them. The key for school leaders in these communities is to not be fooled. The magic comes from not being intimidated by the camouflage.

Students often ask, "You feel me?" The key is to take the risk, step out of our own place of judgment, and just try it. Students do not want the adults to feel *for* them, to operate from a place of sympathy or privilege or saviorism. They want authenticity, because for them, "the shit is real." The duty of the school leader is first to demonstrate authentic interest in young people, to listen and learn and discard self-consciousness in order to interact with them. School leaders need to model genuine curiosity, vulnerability, and a desire to build relationships.

Lamar entered Botello's school mid-year in January of 2017 as a tenth grader who was already seventeen years old. He had been "attending" continuation school (an alternative school setting created for students who have not succeeded at traditional high schools, designed for "contract work" and minimum school day schedules) for the last two years, and during that time, he had earned twenty credits. In two years, he had completed four classes, and no one intervened. No one cared enough to truly help him, and his negative behavior grew out of that treatment.

He was sent to continuation after being kicked out of public high school during his ninth grade year. In his IEP, the Special Education team at his large public high school identified him as "ED," meaning Emotionally Disturbed, due to his violent outbursts and their inability to de-escalate him. He came to AJR, a huge young man, standing over six feet tall, intimidating in his stature and disposition. He knew how to respond to profiling; he knew how to scare teachers and other school personnel. He knew how to get away with doing what he wanted to do in school, which, according to his educational history, was nothing.

What Lamar was not prepared for was being treated like a person; being held accountable to expectations, while being respected and listened to. Ms. Botello and her staff, including administrative staff, faculty, and security, were determined to break down his walls. They would not use a discipline plan or a system, but rather, they would continue to remind themselves and each other to check any implicit biases they might have and to treat Lamar as a student with potential. They would not criminalize him with their attitudes and approaches, but they would continue to work with him and teach him and educate his mind and heart.

Eventually, after several incidents, Ms. Botello passed Lamar's tests and proved to be a real human being who would not judge him by his past. He finally began to trust her and then subsequently the staff of a school he could call his own for the first time in his life. He became academically success-ful—enough to play varsity basketball, which was his passion. He developed a circle of friends and he learned how to be an active, participatory student in his classes. His special education teachers did not baby him or hold him to low expectations. Instead, they supported him academically and socially, and they pushed him to be better. There was simply no trace of the ED label that was given to him at his prior schools.

Lamar wore braids for two years, but he came to school at the start of his senior year with his hair cut neatly in short waves. Botello had never seen him looking so "clean cut." Then, about a month into the school year, Lamar wore a purple wave cap to school. Most African American men wear these "doo rags" only to sleep and then remove them after they style their hair in the morning. Honestly, that was all Botello knew about grooming when it came to African American male hair. She knew he should not be wearing the doo rag at school since it was not part of the school uniform. She had to hold him to the expectations of the community, and she walked up to him.

"Take that off your head!" she told her student quickly in the hallway.

"Ok, miss," he replied and quickly removed it. Later that day, he would have it on his head again, which troubled Ms. Botello, since by now he rarely ignored her requests. They had known each other for two years now, and had built a strong relationship. The next day, Lamar was wearing his wave cap again. It was bright purple, which by this time annoyed the principal. Why wasn't he listening to her? He was making her look like a fool, walking around school, technically out of uniform, flaunting the fact that he didn't have to follow the rules. She momentarily abandoned all of her National Equity Project training and stormed over to him after lunch in the hallway.

"I asked you several times to take that doo rag off your head! Why can't you just listen to me? I can't have everyone here thinking that you don't have to follow the rules! What is wrong with you?!" She was raising her voice in frustration by now, exasperated at having spent so much time building this relationship, only to be disrespected in this way.

"It's cuz I don't have a brush!" He responded in the same exasperated tone she was using with him. "I haven't had one all week! No one will buy me a new one!"

"Oh, ok then," Ms. Botello stopped in her tracks and walked him over to her office. She felt foolish, like she had taken so many steps backward in her efforts to eliminate her implicit biases. She had not even left a door open for the possibility of this particular response. She realized then that no matter how "woke" she liked to think she was, she needed to continually do the work of meeting students where they were. She had to work on herself, not just focus on fixing him. He had literally answered her question and told her what was wrong: he needed a brush and the wave cap helps control his hair—and he needed to trust her to understand his predicament. It was really quite simple, and the next move was critical.

"Let's get you a new brush, then," she said, and then walked over to her computer. Trusty Amazon could do the job quickly.

"Make sure it's hard on one side and soft on the other," Lamar explained. Again, Ms. Botello was being *schooled*—learning that she had so much more to learn. She clicked on the first available dual-sided hairbrushes, "Geoffrey Bean, must be good," she thought. Lamar was approaching her, standing over her shoulder.

"Miss, miss, scroll down!" He exclaimed. "That's like $30!"

"You do it, then" and he began to scroll.

"This one is six, it's good enough." he calmly stated. "Thanks so much, miss." He looked at her genuinely grateful, as if he could not believe his principal would actually help him buy a brush. This was something so simple, such a small gesture, yet to him, something so big.

"Of course, mijo! Now, no more wave caps at school."

"Yes, thanks again."

The brush arrived in two days, and it was done. The problem was solved. He stated the truth. She respected his truth and helped him. They had known each other for two years. They had created a space for honest dialogue and trusted each other's best intentions. There was no criminalization, no punishment, just simple help, which in turn created even more mutual respect.

Ms. Botello acknowledged her own mistakes in judgment and Lamar trusted her enough to ask for help. He didn't wear a wave cap again. And he graduated from high school after five years, winning Most Valuable Player on the basketball team his senior year. He enrolled in LA Southwest College and is currently attending college with his best friend, both with the intention of playing college basketball. That day Ms. Botello took care of a little thing that she came to realize was a pivotal move in making progress with this particular student. Her tenacity with love and respect in a small way was a lever in his sustained transformation.

STEVE AND JUAN: CONFRONT WITH LOVE

Most school leaders and teachers are not trained counselors. It's not what they do. No one should expect them to provide professional counseling to young people, but what transformational leaders do is prepare all the adults in the building—including security guards, teacher's assistants, office staff, and teachers—to be mentors to the young people, who need as much consistent support and guidance as possible in order to persevere through the trauma. These leaders are creative in their ability to leverage the life experiences of all the adults, who provide valuable assets to the team of educators who work with their students every day.

Juan got kicked out of middle school in 2015. His mother still applied to Animo Jackie Robinson and he was accepted via the school lottery. When his middle school principal learned about his acceptance, she came directly to the principal's office and asked her not to accept him because it would be "a danger to the safety of the school complex."

The principal needed to think long and hard about accepting him, but rejecting him would conflict directly with the school's motto: *If you stick with us, we'll stick with you.* She had to acknowledge that every student deserves another chance, especially in the transition between middle school and high school. Juan enrolled in the school and started Summer Bridge, which is a month-long summer program for incoming ninth graders, during the summer of 2015.

Immediately, Juan demonstrated to the Summer Bridge staff the reasons he was a challenging student in middle school. He was rude; he talked out of turn and said what he wanted to say; and he walked in a physically imposing way down the hallway, attempting to intimidate other students. In his English class, the students were doing a gallery walk, where they were supposed to illustrate aspects of their personalities to the other students in an effort to get know each other.

Juan had the nerve to write on his chart, "I hate gays." The teacher wasn't sure if he was trying to get a rise out of him, or if he truly had no problem stating that he didn't like gay people. Rather than jumping all over him, Mr. Ramos simply decided to call someone to cover his class, as he walked Juan to the principal's office. He knew they needed to implement the Restorative Practice of a "harm circle" immediately. The summer staff quickly gathered the administrators, teacher, counselor, parent, and student. They designed a discussion with Juan to teach him the culture of AJR. They needed to message to him that at this school, he could never use that kind of hate speech, and more importantly, they intended to talk with him and listen to him in order to learn why he would say such a thing in the first place.

The circle wasn't meant to be a discipline hearing, but rather a teaching moment for a brand new student. In the circle, the adults explained how people treat each other at this school. They don't belittle people, target people, or disrespect people with words or actions. There is no need for that here. Everyone should feel safe. People should be kind to one another. Juan listened to everyone and then blurted out in a confused tone.

"So, what do you want me to do? Walk down the hallway and just say 'hi' to people?"

"Yes, exactly."

"Umm, hmmm."

"That's what people will do to you."

It was a unified front, clear and unwavering. Just be nice, and everything feels so much better at school. Juan was obviously out of his element. He didn't know how to "just be nice" to people. He was so used to being hard. He masked his insecurities on the daily, angry, mean, making fun of differences. How can he just be open to folks? Kind? Wishing people a nice day? "Impossible," his fourteen-year-old self thought. He left the office and walked down the hall, where students, all older than he, laughed and talked and said, "Good morning" to each other and adults. The principal walked by him and said,

"Good morning, Juan, how are you doing?"

"Good morning. I'm good, you?" He responded. That wasn't so hard and it didn't feel fake, either. He wondered if things would continue to feel different at this school.

That was in his first year, four and a half years ago. Juan ended up playing varsity football all four years. Coach Orange, who was also the Campus Security Officer, pushed him, cared for him, and held him to the highest expectation for grades and character. He implemented physical consequences for Juan and the entire team when Juan got in trouble, which he did—often. His assistant principal, Dr. McDonnell, met with him for thirty minutes a week in his office during advisory class, just to talk and check in and make sure he was keeping up, staying eligible to play, and feeling ok.

The maintenance man, Larry, impressed with his football skills and realizing he needed another man in his life, met with him at lunch, talked to him, bought him cleats. The office assistant, Laura, took him into her circle of students, made sure he had food, called his mom when she needed to. His teachers, especially his special education teachers, supported him with extra time and assistance, while still pushing him to excel in his classes.

The principal made sure he really knew that she was in it for the long haul with him. *Everyone* paid attention to him, when he did well *and* when he messed up, and he learned about asking for help, asking for forgiveness, owning his mistakes, and learning from them. He faltered often, but he never gave up. They wouldn't let him.

At the start of the senior year a tiny, sweet boy named Steve entered as a ninth grade special education student and treated Juan like a hero. He was not physically strong and he spoke in a high voice, almost the voice of a child. He clearly demonstrated feminine characteristics in his stature and in his interactions with others. Juan didn't even think about it. He took Steve into his circle, protected him from potential bullies and made sure everyone at school knew that if they messed with Steve, they would be messing with him, the strongest young man in school.

At the Homecoming game, Steve and his mom made a poster with number forty-three on it, dedicated to his favorite player and friend, Juan, also known as "Biggie." Juan was genuinely humbled and appreciative, and he carried it to the bus after the game, which the team won. Later that year he helped Steve become the water boy for the basketball team, and Steve organically was able to integrate into the school community and avoid any negative interactions with other students. The other students just knew that it was not ok to *press* Steve. That's not how folks at AJR did things.

How did this happen? What transformed Juan from being a bully and perpetrator against any gay student, any small person, any student who for whatever reason felt different or isolated, into a protector of someone so small and easy to target? Botello and the AJR staff are committed to the idea that every student has the potential to "just be nice," because we all innately want to be treated with respect, and when we are, we inevitably treat others in the same way. It feels good to be kind, and it feels safe to be a part of a community.

It becomes easy to care for more than just ourselves, and when we give it, we get it. Over the years, Juan learned this and he continues to live it. It is an ongoing, daily process, but he is literally transforming himself with the help of a community.

Schools need to be safe places to learn. Students need to feel safe, physically, emotionally, socially, in order to even be open to learning. Math and

English, science and history, any academic work doesn't even come into the picture for students, especially those living in poverty and chronic trauma, until relationships begin to grow and develop. In a presentation that Botello attended, esteemed educator, Pedro Noguera, stated that relationships are what truly creates safety in schools, not more security guards, police presence, or metal detectors.

Students feel responsible for the safety of others, when they believe people care about *them* and *their* safety. They begin to care when they feel cared for as human beings. They can trust adults, when adults cease to prejudge and profile them. They can start to learn from adults who simply approach them as if they want to learn, as if they truly have potential to rewrite their own narratives, even when their actions seem to convey the opposite. True transformation takes time, because there are many mistakes to learn from, so lasting relationships matter, and students need personalized attention in order to form those relationships. That's what makes it so difficult, but also so validating for educators.

MIGUEL AND MIGUEL'S PARENTS:
FACILITATE GREATNESS

Like every other high school in poor communities, Animo Jackie Robinson is home to amazing young people who thrive despite overwhelming odds. These students are scholars, activists, artists, and problem-solvers. They somehow leverage their own personal resilience to propel them academically and socially. They excel and thrive, and sometimes school leaders overlook their needs because they seem to have it all together.

Educators focus instead on the students on the fringes, who are barely surviving, because their particular needs are often so urgent and intense, that they demand constant attention. Still, Botello has learned that the best leaders in transformative schools make it a point to notice the student leaders, too, and work to enrich *their* school experience and highlight *their* accomplishments.

They realize that the best students also face overwhelming odds and need support to succeed in the world of college and beyond. It is just as important to fortify the best and brightest as it is to strengthen the most wanting students. In fact, by strengthening the top tier, we create additional mentors for the bottom tier and strengthen the network of support that is critical for all.

Miguel graduated from Animo Jackie Robinson in 2017. He had spent four years excelling in school in all areas. He had a grade point average above 4.0. He had participated in student leadership and was the chair of the Community Service Committee. During his tenth grade year he became involved in the Facing History Student Leadership Group, organizing student events and helping teachers to better understand students' needs and concerns regarding their social emotional health and the community at large.

In his eleventh grade year, Miguel co-founded the Feed the Needy club, determined to support the homeless community surrounding the school. He was able to recruit over twenty students, who then volunteered to serve food at the local Union Rescue Mission on several occasions. He raised funds to host a sandwich drive, where students gathered to make sandwiches and then delivered them to local homeless folks. He raised awareness regarding the homeless issue among students at the high school, as well as among students all over the city. He participated in the mayor's Youth Council in order to garner more support for this issue.

During the summer after his eleventh grade year, he participated in the Global Citizens' Initiative at Harvard University. There he developed his skills in activism and organizing and for his Senior Action Project he was able to fund a mobile shower unit for homeless people in the neighborhood. He raised $5,000 for his project and during senior year had the opportunity to speak at the annual Facing History and Ourselves Benefit Dinner. This is when Ms. Botello and the other staff at AJR found out about Miguel's life at home.

During his speech he explained that he and his family were also homeless for a year. They lived from check to check and his father worked extremely hard to find them a home to live in, so he knew firsthand what it was like to be homeless. His principal was in the audience, and she never knew this fact. How could such a successful, positive student have experienced such trauma without evidence of it ever coming up in his school life? Ms. Botello again was in the shoes of a learner.

During his twelfth grade year he applied to the Posse Scholarship and was awarded a four-year scholarship to UC Berkeley. He chose, instead, to attend Georgetown University, who also awarded him a four-year scholarship. After his first year at Georgetown, he applied for a fellowship in London for the summer and got it. He became a world traveler, a scholar, the first person in his family to venture out into the world and open it up to his family and the future generations to come.

In the spring of 2019, about twenty juniors of Animo Jackie Robinson were given the opportunity to travel to the East Coast of the United States to visit Ivy League and other prestigious universities, and their parents were a bit anxious about allowing them to travel so far away from home, even though the school had raised all the money for the trip. Miguel's tenth grade teacher, Ms. Gonzalez, called his parents, who live ten minutes away from school, to come and speak to the group of current parents.

Their son was in Washington D.C. at the time, but nevertheless, they immediately responded and when they spoke to the parents in their native Spanish, they said everything the other parents needed to hear. They were able to speak directly to them, addressing their concerns and alleviating their fears.

"We need to let them fly," Miguel's father said quietly and poetically in his native tongue. "We need to allow them to see the world and take advantage of all it has to offer." Mr. Gomez described all the things Miguel had learned away from home, everything from small things like cooking and doing laundry, to big things like money management, self-care, and trusting himself. The parents listened calmly, fears assuaged, and they allowed their children to leave home and travel to the East Coast.

The AJR staff recognize the many layers involved in creating a path to college for their students. Just as the young people need to feel safe and supported, their parents also need to be able to trust the people who work with their kids. The community a school builds involves several intersecting rings of people, and those relationships need to be fostered over time. School leaders realize that we empower people in various ways, and providing opportunities for them to *serve* each other is one of the most important ways that we can empower our students and their parents.

We can create opportunities for greatness and we can foster our students' ability to shine, and, even more so, we can create a legacy of greatness in our school communities by being real advocates for our students, as they push themselves beyond the limits that are meant to trap them in their neighborhoods.

ANGEL: CREATE A SAFE SPACE THROUGH VULNERABILITY AND HONESTY

Kristin Botello's vocation is to create a space where a kid can arrive to school as one person and leave having gained something that helps her become an empowered and hopeful individual, even though the "stuff" of his life is still there. To Ms. Botello, the students in these communities have proven to be as intelligent, driven, passionate, and ambitious as the most successful students in every high school in the country.

What makes them special is that on top of this, they are also survivors. In her acclaimed novel, *The House on Mango Street*, Sandra Cisneros refers to "skinny trees," who "grow up and grow down and never quit their anger" (Cisneros 1989). These trees teach her main character not to give up, even when it seems impossible to succeed. The skinny trees give her hope. At AJR students are also "skinny trees," who grow in the middle of a sidewalk, who teach her not to forget to "keep reaching."

Roy came to AJR at the beginning of his eleventh grade year, after having attended a small Catholic all boys' school for his first two years of high school. He was a successful student, quiet and studious, adjusting well to a new school community. He got along well with the other students and teachers. He participated in one club at school, the Gay Straight Alliance (GSA), where, over time, he became a leader.

One year later, during his senior year, Roy came to his GSA friends and adviser, and he shared that he decided to come out to his family and some school staff as a transgender individual. Later that year, Roy decided to come out to the entire staff and student population. She asked to be called "Angel" from then on, and she worked directly with the school psychologist, counselor, teachers, and administration to communicate her message to the school community.

"I had wanted to wait until college to come out as trans, but then I realized that the world is tough and I have to be ready to respond to hate speech, slurs or worse. What better place to share my true identity than here, where I feel safest? You all will help me get prepared for the real world."

When teachers began to call Roy by her new name, Angel, some students had questions and were a bit confused, but no one showed hostility or animosity. The staff had carefully prepared for any possible issues with Angel's transition, but there was not a single conflict. The students simply accepted it. Angel had established a student ally in each of her classes, but there was no need. The rest of the students began to call Angel by her new name and to refer to her with female pronouns.

Later that semester the GSA worked with teachers and other staff members to create advisory lessons for the student body that explored the history of the civil rights movement for the LGBTQI+ community, lessons on bullying, cyber-bullying, and other forms of "otherism." They wanted to educate and illuminate the students with knowledge and learning experiences that would essentially make them better, more respectful, aware human beings. These have been some of the most successful lessons in the advisory curriculum.

Angel has been able to not only navigate her own life with courage and intention, but also provide learning experiences for her school community that have contributed to everyone's individual and collective growth. At Senior Awards Night Angel was awarded the Animo Courage Awards by her faculty, which she accepted with a beaming smile, brighter than any other smile Botello had ever seen on her.

At the school, the administration continues to build in these opportunities for students and staff to contribute to shaping the school culture around relevant issues that can truly make a difference in their community. Angel may not have been Angel in another environment. She may not have felt safe enough. She not only demonstrated her own unbelievable courage, but also pushed the adults and the other students to be brave and to be willing to learn and stretch themselves. By normalizing bravery, the school leaders have created a truly safe space for learning at all levels for their community members.

FAITH: PROTECT FOLKS

When adults working with students who are living in various forms of trauma, honor them and honor their struggle, the students begin to take on a different attitude toward it. They begin to harness their pain as a form of strength, and, as Vietnam veteran and US senator, Max Cleland, wrote in his memoir, they become "strong at the broken places" (2000). Helping students to leverage their trauma to fortify them to reach for higher heights is one part of Ms. Botello's purpose. Her goal is not to save kids' lives, but rather to enable them to save their *own* lives by forging new paths.

Faith is under five feet tall and she weighs about ninety pounds soaking wet. She is tiny. She has always been tiny. When she was a seventh grade student at the co-located middle school that shares a campus with AJR, she looked like she was ten years old. She came up to Ms. Botello and told her, "I'm coming to your school in two years!" her mouth wide and eyes bright. Indeed, she came to AJR in 2015 and she thrived. She was the kind of student that teachers loved to have in class, because she was always happy and always prepared for class, and she was naturally curious and inquisitive. She was what teachers frequently call "a joy to have in class."

In her tenth grade year, Faith and her older brother were at the bus stop near the school at about 6:00 pm. It was winter and already dark. The family regularly experienced instability and trauma. Dad was in and out of jail, and mom was trying to keep it together. She had recently moved them about fifteen miles away from school to a distant community in East Los Angeles. Faith was scared, but she had Bryan, so she felt confident that they would be okay. Suddenly, a car stopped at the bus stop. The woman in the passenger seat asked them a question.

"Do you know what time it is?" Faith had her brand new IPhone in her hand. She had worked at the park all summer to earn enough money to buy it for just under $600. She looked at her phone and answered the woman.

"It's six." Meanwhile, the man in the driver's seat got out of the car, quickly walked around it and grabbed the phone out of her hand. He pushed her to the ground and ran back to get into the car. Faith's brother, Bryan, ran after the man and tried to get her phone back. There was a scuffle, but the guy was able to get back into the car and the couple drove away. The siblings were angry and terrified, and they called their mother. The night of going to the police station, reporting the crime, finally getting home was long and arduous, and the next morning, mom came to the office to report the crime and share her concerns with the staff.

"It's too dangerous, here. I know that the kids love their school, and I know you do your best, but you can't keep them safe. Once Jonathan graduates, I can't keep Faith here. I'm going to have to transfer her out. There's no way I can pick her up, so I have no other choice." Faith was sobbing. The last thing she wanted to do was leave the school, but she had absolutely no say and no power to change her mom's mind. She was simply too small to protect herself on the streets and she lived too far to get home on her own.

Ms. Laura was the office assistant in the main office and had developed a close relationship with Faith over the last two years. Faith loved Ms. Laura and Ms. Laura took care of her. Ms. Botello knew she had to solve the problem. She had to guarantee some form of safety and protection for this young lady in order for her mother to even consider letting her stay. Ms. Laura spoke to the principal.

"What if we take her home? What if we drive her?" Laura offered to mom. "We both drive that way on our way home. It might be a little later, but we can get her home safely."

"I can do two days and Ms. Laura can do the other three." Ms. Botello added. "What if we promise that she will never have to take the bus home alone? Can she stay then?" Faith's mother thought about it. She would let them know. By the end of the year, Faith's mom decided that she would allow Faith to stay at AJR as long as she got home safely.

Faith stayed for two more years. Ms. Laura and Ms. Botello drove her home every day and she was able to keep her grades up, despite numerous challenges at home. She maintained her positivity, even in the face of relentless trauma. In her senior year she was elected as the Associated Student Body president and she even became prom queen.

She worked every summer, continued to strive to achieve her goals and participated in the Facing History Student Leadership Group to learn about global issues and work to spread awareness and facilitate change in the school community. She applied and was accepted at several universities, including UC Berkeley, where she decided to attend. On the way home, Ms. Botello and Faith often discussed what could have happened if Faith had left their school.

"Imagine, miss, where would I have been without you guys?"

"I don't know, mija, but I'm so glad you're here. I have a question for you. You see, I'm about to write this article about our school. How would you describe it? What do you think makes us different?" The young woman thought for a few minutes and came up with an answer.

"You guys give us hope," she stated simply, but profoundly. Ms. Botello realized that Faith taught her more than she could ever teach Faith about the human capacity for not only survival, but redefinition. Her success reinforced Botello's belief that love manifested in small yet significant ways is truly transformational.

Faith is still tiny, but she is also so big. Ms. Botello and other staff members, as well as her friends, helped her survive the drug abuse and multiple arrests and jail sentences of her parents. They helped her survive hunger and instability and lack of resources, but, in truth, she is the person who really did it.

She did exactly what the school was created for her to do—she leveraged her own resilience, creativity, and intelligence, which has helped survive her adolescence—in order to embrace the unknown challenge of college. She developed enough self-love, even in the midst of impossible odds, to believe she could go to college, and she achieved her goal. This young woman and hundreds like her consistently provide Ms. Botello with the proof and the motivation to continue in their work.

SYLVIA AND ANDREA: EVERYTHING MATTERS—CONSISTENT CARE

In schools where complex, generational trauma is prevalent, all students, including both high-performing students and struggling students, have a story to tell. Sometimes adults know their stories and oftentimes they are not aware of them. It is erroneous to assume that the students who are displaying behavioral challenges are the only students who are struggling at home. School leaders sometimes make the mistake of overlooking the indicators of trauma that may be present among their highest performing students. This was the case for Sylvia.

What does it mean to be homeless? What does it feel like when you have to keep going to school, keep studying, keep being a daughter, a big sister, a cheerleader, knowing you have to go home to a place that isn't a home? Sylvia and her family lost their home when their father lost his job and they couldn't afford to pay rent. She was in the tenth grade, and her older sister was in her second year at UCLA. They were both amazing students, successful in school and active student body leaders. Allison couldn't stop attending college, or she would lose her scholarship.

She had received a full four-year scholarship to UCLA, and she knew she couldn't waste her opportunity, even though her family needed her so desperately in the present. She lived at the university and came home every weekend to help the family in any way she could. Sylvia didn't skip a beat in school, and if folks didn't know her so well, they wouldn't know she was living in a small motel on Broadway, with her three younger siblings and her mother. Both girls got jobs and worked on the weekends and their mother did all she could doing piecework in a local sweatshop. How were they ever going to make it?

The beauty of attending Animo Jackie Robinson for them was that they knew they had people to rely on in a community outside of their immediate family. They could ask for help. They didn't have to be ashamed of their situation, and they weren't alone.

One weekend before Christmas Ms. Botello was getting her hair done, when her hairdresser, Sonia, mentioned that she wanted to do something special for her holiday charity.

"Have you heard on Snapchat that folks do this Adopt-a-family charity?"

"I don't know about that, but I know a family that you could help if you want to."

"Yes!" Sonia replied. "What they do is they give the family Christmas. They get gifts for everyone in the family and other supplies, etc." Ms. Botello described the Flores family and explained their extreme need. They were the perfect family for Sonia to help. When Ms. Botello mentioned to Sylvia that someone outside of AJR, but connected to her, wanted to help, Sylvia was humbled and grateful.

"Ok, miss, thank you so much!" She shared that her mother, little sister, and brothers would be very appreciative of any kind of Christmas that she could provide.

Later that month, Sonia had gathered a list of the family's needs and acquired the presents for them. Ms. Botello arranged for the family to come to her home and meet with Sonia. When she arrived, she brought a carload of gifts for the family. She set everything up to look and feel special, and then the family arrived in their Honda Civic. There were five kids, the youngest was 3 and the oldest was 20, and their mother. They were quietly polite, gracious, and filled with gratitude. Their mother was almost speechless in her humility and the small children were giddy with joy at the sight of their presents.

"Do you want to open one?" Sonia asked.

"Puedo, mama?" the youngest girl, Cinthia, asked. Her mother obliged and the three small children opened one gift each. Cinthia was shocked at the *Hello Kitty* bus she received. She was overwhelmed with excitement. The two boys were similarly thrilled with their toys. They didn't know that Sylvia had given Sonia a list of their interests and so they were shocked with excitement as they opened gifts that they immediately loved. Sonia couldn't contain her joy. She had no idea that she was going to be personally affected and so emotional in the moment. Her bright eyes filled with tears, and she couldn't contain her smile.

"Thank you for everything. There are no words to describe how much we thank you. May God bless you." The mother kept repeating, as she held Sonia's face in her hands. She hugged her tightly, and little Cinthia couldn't stop crying.

"Why are you crying?" Sonia asked.

"I don't know." Cinthia nodded her head, as she continued to sob, hugging her big sister's leg.

"Do you want to hug Sonia?" Ms. Botello asked, and Cinthia quickly nodded her head. She didn't know what she was feeling, but she was feeling so much that she couldn't contain herself. She hugged Sonia tightly and Sonia, too, became overwhelmed.

"Thank you, thank you!" Cinthia kept saying.

"No, thank *you*," Sonia repeated to the family and to Ms. Botello. "You have given *me* so much." A month prior to this day, she had planned to be a force of good that changed the lives of a family in need, but she didn't realize that they would be changing her life. She walked them to their car, and said good-bye, only to remember them forever.

How is this story relevant to growing a school culture and battling the relentless suffering of the ghetto? How can a school fight homelessness? In truth, it can't. What it can do, though, is provide authentic care, community, and humanity in the midst of a society that often strips its people of all of these things.

Ms. Botello knows that all the little things are big for the students in her school and their families. In fact, the little things are so big, that they sometimes matter more than the large, public moves. Small acts can be more impactful for students than larger acts, because they are more authentic to them. They believe us when we say we are here for them. They believe us when we say we believe in them and when we tell them that they can and will make it to and through college. And when they really believe it, they work that much harder for what they so desperately want.

Eight months later, the Flores family is still homeless and still struggling week to week, but their school family is also still supporting them in small and big ways, and that can't happen everywhere.

Ms. Botello realized that a huge part of running her school in her community is care. Leaders must prioritize caring for their students and their adults. They must notice. They must listen and observe without judgment. Most importantly, they must be approachable and trustworthy. Students often need small things, like snacks and water, or a uniform sweater; and they also need big things, like help getting housing or a link to resources that could change a major aspect of their lives.

And they don't stop needing help after graduation. At Animo Jackie Robinson, the leaders and staff ensure that their students are willing and able to seek help from them in order to thrive in school and beyond.

CONCLUSION: RADICAL IMAGINING

For school leaders who serve the most overlooked populations of students in communities neglected by most of society, it may seem radical to imagine school transformation rooted in love. Leaders may be looking for blueprints of curriculum, instruction, or behavior management, for programs focused on transforming learning habits, or structuring school systems, but Botello's radical imagining asserts that authentic, relational leadership makes everyone at the school better. People who are treated as human beings who want to improve, actually do improve—and that includes adults and students.

Strong leaders *can* root their work in love. They don't have to be afraid to be vulnerable. They can model authentic learning from mistakes and they can create an alternative narrative of leadership as service and care for adults who work with and for their students. They can imagine, *What if everyone at school really believed that another person (or many people) had faith in them? What if everyone felt elevated by the work they did? What if we all, regularly, in the words of her art teacher, Rachel, "lifted each other up"?*

What could students achieve if they truly embraced the fact that they could make mistakes and learn from them? If they internalized confidence and hope instead of cynicism? If they felt valued by and accountable to someone they cared for? If they could actually *see* a better future? Wouldn't they work for it?

Kristin Botello understands that it is radical to be an idealist in the belly of the beast. It's radical to keep believing, when the boulders of disappointment, tragedy, institutionalized racism and oppression, and low performance continue to roll down that mountain upon schools in the inner city. But Botello has been an educator in East and South Los Angeles for thirty years. She has been leading Animo Jackie Robinson for the last thirteen years, even though not one of those years has been easy.

People often ask her, "How can you do this work for so long?" For Botello, the answer lies in the concept of servant leadership. Botello contends that true empowerment comes from *service*, and this work, the work of transformational leadership in urban schools, is the most honorable form of service, leading to her self-actualization. She and other leaders working and living in the belly of the beast ask themselves, "Am *I* served by this work? Does it feed *me*? Is this specific work something *I* need in order to feel that I am living *my* purpose?" and for them the answer is yes.

They believe that it is their responsibility and privilege to serve their students and participate in their transformation, because that transformation is intertwined with their own ongoing redefinition. Often educators in the ghetto confuse service with saving someone else, but the truth for Botello is that the work, the real work, is part of her journey of self-preservation and self-love. It keeps her alive and thriving and growing, and she has no intention of stopping.

REFLECTIVE QUESTIONS FOR LEADING
IN THE BELLY OF THE BEAST

1. At your school site, how can individual transformation lead to collective or community transformation? What would be some productive steps to begin this process?
2. Reflect on the concept that paradigm shifts in self-concept for students in poverty can lead to transformation and ultimately a student's ability to rewrite their own narratives? What is the responsibility of adults at the school to facilitate this shift?
3. What is the difference between authentic relationship building and trivial or staged moves that educators may make in the name of "building positive school cultures"?
4. Reflect on the paradox of putting students first while putting teachers first.
5. Choose one of the stories presented by Ms. Botello and reflect on the message for educators that the story illustrates.

Chapter 4

The Freedom to Think Critically

Meredith Gavrin

It wasn't until I was given intellectual freedom that I was able to grow as a teacher and take pride in being an educator.

—Marco Cenabre, teacher

INTRODUCTION

High school mission statements across the nation use many of the same phrases; they promise to teach their students to "think critically and analytically"; to provide a "rigorous" and "innovative" education; and to prepare students to "make insightful judgments," "problem solve effectively," be "empowered," or "thoughtful" citizens. At the same time, the teachers charged with these challenges often operate under directives that smother their critical thinking about their own instruction, discourage them from innovating, and fail to empower them. They typically receive one-size-fits-all professional development, are required to follow curriculum centrally designed and prescribed by their districts, and, in increasing numbers, are given lesson scripts to follow.

These initiatives not only stifle innovation and creativity, but also come from a place of inherent distrust for teachers as professionals. If a school intends to graduate students who think critically and problem-solve in all the ways those mission statements promise, then the educators who instruct, inspire, and lead them to those desired ends must be empowered and resourced to do so on a daily basis as well.

In 2015, *Ed Week* asked teachers to respond to the question, "Why Do Some Teachers Stay at Difficult-to-Staff Schools?" In her response, educator

79

Katy Farber—also the author of the book *Why Great Teachers Quit and How We Might Stop the Exodus*—explains that teachers who leave the classroom cite "limited growth opportunities" and "a competitive, isolating and controlling standardized test culture" among their reasons; in contrast, Opal Davis Dawson lists "professional learning, ongoing collaboration, staff resources . . . and shared decision making" among the reasons teachers *stay*.[1]

In another similar piece, published in *The Washington Post,* teacher Alice Trosclair writes, "In no other profession is a college-educated individual questioned, second-guessed, and blamed as much as teachers. The media slams teachers while parents, principals, and central office workers question their abilities."[2]

An expert teacher in an urban school has countless skills and has to think on many levels at once:

- She plans units that account not only for the content her students will learn about but also for the skills they must master and the ways they will demonstrate that mastery.
- She builds in checkpoints along the way that provide her with information about how her students' understanding is progressing, and she has to build in reteaching opportunities for students who are struggling.
- She has to bear in mind those students in the room who need modified assignments or extra supports and accommodations according to their Individualized Education Plans under special education law.
- She has English language learners who may have sophisticated understanding of the concepts but need modified texts or supports during instruction to access the information.
- She has some students who walked into the classroom in the morning after helping younger siblings get to school or after checking on elderly family members before getting to school themselves.
- She has students who experienced violence in their neighborhoods or have family members under threat of deportation.
- She has students who transferred into the school two weeks prior or may know they're leaving two weeks hence.
- She has students who, along with their mothers and siblings, are currently sleeping in the living room of a cousin's home or at a nearby shelter.
- She bears in mind the cultural, ethnic, and socioeconomic diversity of her group of students.
- And she is preparing all of them to be successful in college, because their access to higher education is critical and pivotal.

Teachers develop their craft and become experts over time, so retaining talented teachers for years matters. For students whose lives are frequently disrupted by other factors, and for teachers whose schools are under-resourced in other ways, it matters urgently.

Meredith Gavrin is the co-founder of New Haven Academy, an Interdistrict Magnet School in New Haven, Connecticut, and has served on the administrative team there since the school's inception in 2003. She met her husband (the school's co-founder), Greg Baldwin, when both were teachers at the Institute for Collaborative Education, a New York City "start-up" public school, in the mid-1990s. The two moved to New Haven in 1999, and they started New Haven Academy in collaboration with the New Haven Public Schools, under the leadership of then-superintendent Dr. Reginald Mayo, and through a state Interdistrict Magnet School grant. The school now serves 290 students in grades ninth to twelfth.

As an "interdistrict magnet," New Haven Academy is a public school of choice and functions as part of the state's efforts to address issues of segregation; New Haven Academy, like other interdistrict magnet schools in New Haven, draws approximately 65 percent of its student body from the City of New Haven and the other 35 percent from any of the twenty-five surrounding suburban communities.

The student population is approximately 65 percent African American, 25 percent Latinx, 2 percent Asian, and 8 percent white, with approximately 70 percent of students qualifying for free and reduced lunch. Students choose New Haven Academy through a district-run lottery process, and there are no criteria for admission—so students represent a wide range of educational backgrounds and levels of skill, and they come from a wide range of middle schools.

In this chapter, Gavrin will describe four ways in which teachers must be allowed to think critically: in *designing engaging curriculum*; in *risk-taking for innovative instruction*; in *receiving differentiated professional development* that accounts for their professional strengths and needs; and in *discussing as a staff the controversial issues of the day* in order to be informed, thoughtful citizens themselves. When teachers are allowed to develop as creative, thoughtful, intellectually engaged professionals, their classrooms become places where student creativity, critical thinking, and intellectual rigor thrive.

DESIGNING ENGAGING CURRICULUM

Gavrin is often asked what she looks for when she interviews teaching candidates. Among many skills and experiences she hopes to find, she particularly values candidates who demonstrate infectious enthusiasm for the discipline they teach. At New Haven Academy, teachers have to not only love teaching, they have to love *what* they teach. In order to find that trait, she often asks teaching candidates, "if you were given the opportunity to design a semester-long elective, what would you teach? Of all the topics in your field, what do you get most excited about?"

This is not an idle question. At New Haven Academy, students (particularly in the eleventh and twelfth grades) have the opportunity to select electives that teachers have designed independently. These courses are, of course, vetted by department colleagues in order to make sure they fall within the department's mission and guidelines for student outcomes in that field, and colleagues help one another design shared assessments across the electives' specific areas of focus.

Inevitably, these electives have become the sites of teachers' most exemplary instruction and students' most engaged learning. Here are three examples from New Haven Academy's course offerings:

- *People and Place*, a history elective designed by Peter Kazienko, explores the impact of geography and geographical changes on social trends and historic events. Units include a study of the death of oystering in New Haven's history, the impact of the damming of the Columbia River on Native Americans in the Pacific Northwest, and the impact of environmental challenges on culture in Japan; in the end of the course, students apply their skills and knowledge to a new case study using maps, documents, and secondary sources.
- *Madness in Literature*, a course designed by Marco Cenabre, has students read literary texts through the lens of mental health and seminal psychological texts. In one unit, students read *The Catcher in the Rye* and study Holden Caulfield's actions and words through a frame of Freudian analysis, breaking down the inner workings of his unconscious throughout the novel, ultimately drafting an essay that analyzes the influence of a specific tension, or stressor, in relation to the character's words and actions. Using differentiated texts and a variety of tools to support their writing, Cenabre enables students across a wide spectrum of skills and reading levels to access this material together.
- In *Anatomy and Physiology*, a science elective designed by David Herndon, students are ultimately assessed on their ability to diagnose a human pathology and demonstrate their understanding through animal dissection. In order to achieve this goal, students present the body system that is mainly affected by the pathology they're studying, explaining how the system will change if the pathology takes hold in a "gallery-style" demonstration to fellow students and visiting adults.

Each of these teachers, like all teachers at New Haven Academy, also follows district curricular guidelines to teach core classes that more closely mirror those taught by their district counterparts. But Gavrin and Baldwin believe in reminding teachers of this mantra: *we hired you because we believe in your expertise in your field and your teaching skills; you should make informed decisions based on what you know works best with your students in your classroom.*

The teachers described above, and others like them who develop engaging courses based on their intellectual interests, typically spend six months to a year developing the course before teaching it for the first time. They read, consult similar course syllabi from other high schools and from universities, have conversations with colleagues within and outside of our staff, and often participate in professional development activities outside of the school in order to further their own learning as they developed their courses.

This level of professional learning not only benefits the new courses, but also serves to deepen their knowledge base and their instructional strategies in all of the courses they teach. When asked to name their favorite classes and—more importantly—the courses in which they had learned the most, felt the most prepared for college, and had performed at their best—New Haven Academy students most often cite these and other electives.

Providing room for innovation in the classroom does not mean thwarting district guidelines—it means finding opportunities and taking them. Gavrin and Baldwin identify course areas where the district requires students to earn credit but does not mandate the course sequence—primarily in eleventh and twelfth grades. Within those areas, they identify course descriptions that match the broad outlines of the courses New Haven Academy teachers want to develop and teach. Finally, within those guidelines, Gavrin and Baldwin give their teachers the freedom to develop and propose the new courses—and hold each of those teachers and their courses to New Haven Academy's standards of academic rigor, engagement of students across skill levels, project-based assessment, and opportunities for students to reflect about their own learning.

In ninth and tenth grade courses (and in some upper level required courses), New Haven Academy follows the broad curricular guidelines provided by the school district. Those guidelines are, in most disciplines, content pacing guides—what topics to cover, in what order, for how much time. However, Gavrin and Baldwin push teachers to follow the Coalition of Essential Schools principle of "less is more"—rather than teaching broad survey courses that race through every topic in a shallow way, teachers thoughtfully identify the units that are most important and delve deeply into *those* topics and skills.

A 2018 Gallup Poll of teachers who left, or considered leaving, the classroom found that "when talented, high-performing employees are not engaged in their job, they are just as likely as disengaged, low performers to quit their job. To engage teachers, leaders must provide a path for them to follow to boost their development, have creativity and autonomy in the classroom, and create a thriving learning environment for students."[3]

Samantha Leska is a teacher who started her career at New Haven Academy. After two years, she moved away to pursue her master's degree; when she returned to Connecticut, she initially worked at a high school that is part of a large charter network. As a teacher in that network, she was given a curriculum with specific requirements and was told how to pace her lessons. When she was told that the next step was that the network would begin to give the teachers *scripted* lesson plans to follow verbatim, she decided to leave. She explains:

> When you do that to teachers, you're inherently saying, "I don't trust you, and I don't trust your judgment." And I think that there is so much of that already in the profession, that the last thing we need is to trust teachers and their judgment even less. I mean, you're talking about a group of people a majority of whom have a masters' degree in this content, and this work, and to give them a daily "to do list" feels so demeaning . . . . I didn't come into a profession to feel like I had to check boxes every day. I came into it because I like the creativity that's involved in it, and if you do that to teachers you take away their creativity, you take away their sense of professionalism, and I don't know who wants that. That's not going to keep people around.[4]

In order to become experts, teachers need to stay in the classroom; in order to stay in the classroom, teachers need to be nurtured and trusted as skilled professionals.

RISK-TAKING FOR INNOVATIVE INSTRUCTION

Many schools indicate, in their mission statements and descriptions of their guiding principles, that they want to graduate students who know how to think critically and solve problems. In order to produce graduates with these skills, we know that we need to give students opportunities to practice throughout their learning. That kind of instruction requires creativity, and it requires modeling in the classroom. If we want our students to think critically and solve problems effectively, then teachers also need to be allowed to innovate, falter, reflect, and redesign their instruction.

The extreme example of undervaluing and undermining teachers' own critical thinking is schools that give strict mandates about instruction or provide scripted lessons to follow. In a moving op-ed in *The Washington Post* in 2013, teacher Valerie Strauss wrote:

I can't do projects with my students anymore because I have to teach the curriculum word-for-word, and I am only allowed to use standards-based assessments (which I must create myself). It doesn't matter how my students learn best . . . . It doesn't matter that my students arrive at my door with a host of factors that I cannot control . . . their home situations, their former schooling, their attitudes toward school and learning and themselves, the neighborhood they live in, whether they are English Language Learners or have special needs, or whether they have just broken up with their girlfriend in the cafeteria. All those factors also affect student performance, but none of that matters. What matters is how my students perform on the state test. (And I must STOP teaching for 6 weeks in the spring to make sure our students pass that test.)[5]

In another essay that describes the impact of a scripted curriculum on a young teacher with whom he worked closely, University of Georgia professor Peter Smagorinsky wrote,

To a teacher who finds planning to be highly stimulating, exciting, enjoyable, and fulfilling, teaching a centrally designed instructional script is immensely frustrating. Like the reduction of real kids to test scores, the implementation of a scripted curriculum takes the engaging, interpersonal, relational career of teaching and reduces it to mechanical operation.[6]

Allowing and encouraging teachers to try innovative teaching strategies in the classroom treats them instead like action researchers. Innovation in the classroom is not the same as "experimenting." No student is going to receive a placebo while others receive effective instruction—but teachers have to have space to try a strategy, lesson, or assessment, explore their results, receive feedback, reflect and redesign, and it has to be okay to falter. Not fail.

If schools clearly articulate the learning standards that students have to master, then they can empower teachers to develop alternative, engaging ways to work on those standards. Here is an example: at New Haven Academy, students in a Literature elective studied the novel *Frankenstein*. The ongoing goal was for students to show mastery of using evidence from the novel to support an argument. They had, throughout the year, worked on that skill in the context of writing argumentative essays.

But in this unit, the teacher, Leszek Ward, tried something different: the students put Dr. Frankenstein on trial for the destruction the monster had caused over the course of the novel. Each student was assigned a role as an attorney or witness, and together in teams, they mined the novel's pages for evidence to support their argument. Students prepared and submitted written opening and closing statements and witness testimony. Other staff members were brought in to serve as the jury on the day of the trial, and the outside adult presence elevated students' engagement and level of academic performance.

In another example, New Haven Academy's biology teacher, David Herndon, required students to prepare and present "TED Talks" about DNA, holding students to rigorous expectations of content accuracy, clarity of explanation, providing a visual model, answering spontaneous questions from the audience, and connecting the concepts to other concepts they had covered in related units.

When the school district determines that the only way to maintain classroom standards is to mandate the format of instruction or the mode of assessment, these opportunities for teachers to develop alternative ways of engaging, instructing, and assessing their students become impossible. Urban school districts often report low performance on mandated testing—and often blame the teachers for the results (or in some districts, tie teacher evaluation and even compensation to those results).

But if the instruction, the tests, and the testing timetable are all driven by external mandates rather than being designed by the teachers who know the students and observe their day-to-day learning, the data from those tests do not give us any meaningful information. Most times the mandated tests have not even been thoughtfully aligned to the mandated curriculum, much less aligned to student needs and strengths.

Marco Cenabre, the teacher who designed the "Madness in Literature" course described above, worked in other urban public schools before coming to New Haven Academy. He explains the impact of different professional expectations and regulations this way:

> Working in other environments, I was given a rigid set of guidelines of what to teach, how to teach, and a specific set of numeric goals I should hit by the end of the year. Working under this structure, my thoughts were limited to sifting through content, planning bloated lessons in order to reach nebulous benchmarks, all within an impossibly small time frame. Although I was able to find success, my students learned to listen and obey in contrast to actually thinking. As an educator, I became adept at getting kids to grow by doing, in contrast to pushing them to grow by doing, thinking and reflecting.

Where he found that rigid, test-score-driven directives stifled his and his students' learning, at New Haven Academy he found that his own opportunities to think deeply about his work allowed him to focus more on his students' actual needs and growth:

> It wasn't until I was given intellectual freedom that I was able to grow as a teacher, and take pride in being an educator. Being given permission shifted

my mindset more towards "Am I meeting my students' needs?" in contrast to, "Am I implementing my curriculum correctly?" This shift alone allowed me the safety to think creatively, escaping rigid guidelines that were not created for the students in my room. As a reflective practitioner, when a student succeeds in the objectives of my lesson, I can thoughtfully adjust and also think about more possibilities of intervention. Intellectual freedom opened my mind for more possibility, allowed me to actualize my own intelligence, and in turn, I now have the mental space to think about my students' individualized needs.[7]

The innovative teachers Gavrin works with, like Cenabre, honed their skills over time. They were able to innovate not only because of the support and license they were given to do so, but also in collaboration with other experienced colleagues, planning together in weekly department meetings and sharing best practices in faculty meetings and in peer-led Professional Learning Groups. But, as we all know, not all teachers are in a place where they are at the stage of innovating and creating in their classrooms.

At New Haven Academy, the experience and capacity of their teachers ranges from those described above to newer teachers who are doing all they can to structure their lessons for the next day and keep their students in their seats and engaged for an entire class period. Therefore, Gavrin and Baldwin also need to design learning experiences that meet all teachers where they are, starting with making sure their newest teachers understand and embody the school's foundational principles.

RECEIVING DIFFERENTIATED
PROFESSIONAL DEVELOPMENT

Here is the story of the Sock Puppet Conference.

Once, as part of a grant the school district had received, a team of administrators was sent to a conference led by the grant-making institution. The conference was held on the last day of school, so the educators in attendance were missing the students' closing activities for the year in order to be there.

One goal of instruction at the conference that day was for the educators participating in the grant to understand a key concept of design—the idea that people need to account for the client or user when they redesign something, and by extension, education reform should account for the needs and interests of the students during the redesign process. It's an important concept.

In order to teach the attendees this concept, however, the conference leaders chose to engage everyone in an activity that included pairing up; discussing their partner's "ideal wallet"; designing that wallet on paper; gathering materials from a table to create that wallet out of construction paper, scotch tape, ziploc bags, magic markers, and stickers; meeting with one's partner to explain the wallet that had been designed; receiving feedback from the partner "client"; and ultimately reflecting on that process.

The activity took at least ninety minutes, and the takeaway was delivered as precisely what was described at the start: bear in mind your user's needs when you redesign. The roomful of educators—absent from the final day of the year in their school buildings—was livid at the condescension and waste of time. (In retelling this story over the years, the wallets apocryphally became sock puppets, and the event was thereafter referred to as the Sock Puppet Conference.)

Professional development should never waste an educator's time. That time would otherwise be spent with or in direct preparation for students, so the bar is high for measuring whether an alternative activity is meaningful enough to replace that. The 2018 Gallup Poll reported, "many teachers might not have felt challenged in their work or received individualized opportunities to grow and advance, so they left their job. Even though many districts invest heavily in professional development programs, these opportunities might not be individualized to teachers' specific growth and development needs."[8]

One organization that meets this bar is *Facing History and Ourselves*, an organization that has partnered with New Haven Academy since its founding and serves as a model for professional development. Facing History's teacher professional development activities honor Trevor Gardner's core value of "Teacher and Learner."

In a typical Facing History teacher seminar, teachers engage directly with challenging historical case studies through close examination of primary sources and head-on discussions of challenging issues including racism, prejudice, genocide, inequity, and bystander behavior. Rather than being able to maintain a critical distance, as often happens in teacher professional development when teachers spend their time discussing their students and *their* "issues," a teacher in a Facing History seminar *becomes* the student.

Only at the end of a challenging series of days, immersed in deep thinking, writing, and conversation about the issues, does a teacher step back to consider how best to bring the material to her own students. Moreover, Facing History recognizes that the professional development can't end there; the organization connects teacher participants with a Facing History program associate who, on an ongoing basis, helps a teacher navigate questions of how to integrate the material and the methods into other curriculum mandates and obligations, or assists a teacher in figuring out how to respond to issues of bias or prejudice that arise among students.

This approach to professional development bears results: A 2015 "Randomized Controlled Trial of Professional Development," a study of Facing History's impact, revealed:

Intervention teachers showed significantly greater self-efficacy in all eight assessed domains, more positive perceptions of professional support, satisfaction and growth, and greater personal accomplishment. Intervention students demonstrated stronger skills for analyzing evidence, agency, and cause and effect on an historical understanding performance measure; greater self-reported civic efficacy and tolerance for others with different views; and more positive perceptions of the classroom climate and the opportunities afforded for engaging with civic matters.[9]

Facing History and Ourselves has been fully integrated into both the curriculum and professional development at New Haven Academy since the school's inception. Every teacher at New Haven Academy attends a Facing History seminar (no matter their teaching discipline) within their first year or two at the school, and the whole staff together participates in professional development with a Facing History staff member once a year.

New Haven Academy also tries to provide opportunities within regular, ongoing professional development to recognize different needs among teachers. Teachers participate in professional development in four ways: individually, through classroom observations and individual meetings with administrators; weekly, in a scheduled meeting with their department colleagues; biweekly, in peer-led "Professional Learning Groups" (PLGs); and twice monthly, in whole-faculty meetings led by administrators. Like all teachers in the New Haven Public Schools, New Haven Academy's teachers also attend district-wide professional development in their discipline once each quarter.

It is relatively easy to adapt individual coaching time to teachers' different needs; by their nature, meetings before and after classroom observations respond directly to one teacher's performance and struggles. What is important, however, is making sure that the time spent with that teacher includes *listening* to the teacher. Gavrin and Baldwin often emphasize questions that include before a lesson, *What are you trying? Why? What do you expect to see? How will you know if students are "getting it"?* And afterward, *What do you think of how it went? What would you change, or will you change before the next class? Now that you've done that, what are you going to do next?*

Just as the school emphasizes metacognition—opportunities for students to think about their own thinking—teachers learn from thinking through their choices in the classroom as well. The conversation does not stop there, but it provides an opportunity for Gavrin and Baldwin to point out what they observe and what they advise in response to the teacher's own reasoning and reflection.

At New Haven Academy, department meetings are collaborative, and Baldwin specifically designs teachers' schedules to enable departments to share a common planning period each week. In a small school in which no department is larger than five people, weekly department time provides opportunities for teachers to share best practices, develop shared tools for instruction and instructional routines, align course work across grades nine through twelve, and coordinate instruction if they share a course with a colleague.

There is even differentiation across departments. Each department must ultimately create (and revise as needed) a department mission statement that aligns with the school's mission statement, a shared electronic file of instructional tools, homework templates, and sample assessments that align with the department's mission, and a shared departmental rubric for grading assessments. These provide guidelines and parameters within which teachers have freedom to create lessons and materials.

But in any given week (or school year), the focus of a department's work will vary depending on how many members of the department are new to the school or new to teaching, how many members of the department are teaching courses that are new to them, or what particular new challenges have arisen as external demands like district guidelines or standardized testing changes require internal adjustments.

PLGs at New Haven Academy are led by three teachers who have trained in facilitation protocols. PLGs began as a commitment the school had to make under a grant it received, but the positive feedback from a range of teachers left Gavrin and Baldwin determined to continue them. The three PLG leaders meet as a team at the start of each semester to identify goals and areas of focus that align with the school's identified professional development needs that year.

Teachers rank their preferences among the PLG groups' areas of focus; one year, they chose among a PLG that used filmed observations from each group member's classrooms, one that examined and critiqued lesson plans, and one that worked on honing project-based assessments. Each time the group meets, one member presents his work, and the group follows and established protocol for exploring the work and providing feedback.

Administrators stay out of these groups entirely so that the groups can be fully candid without worry of any evaluative component. Because each member brings her own work to the table, the meeting responds to her identified needs; because the group follows a protocol, the routine keeps the time focused and productive.

Finally, whole-faculty professional development time strives to be responsive to different needs as well. Faculty meetings are designed with some of the same principles that guide high-quality teaching. In preparing for faculty time, Gavrin and Baldwin ask themselves:

• What is the tangible goal—what will teachers come out of the meeting having practiced or created? How does this meeting's goal build toward our larger goals for the year?

- How will they participate actively during the meeting?
- How do we want to group teachers during the work time—in departments, or across departments? Within groups that share similar strengths and weaknesses, or across them?
- After the meeting, how will we follow up to make sure the work transfers back to the classroom?

As often as they can, Gavrin and Baldwin build in time during each meeting for teachers to apply the topic of the day to their own instruction, leaving the meeting with a planned strategy to use in the classroom that week, or an adjustment to their lesson plans, or an idea to implement during an upcoming unit.

Faculty meetings are also critical times for teachers to talk about the world and the many ways it enters their classrooms.

DISCUSSING AS A STAFF THE CONTROVERSIAL ISSUES OF THE DAY

For years, Gavrin took for granted that the staff she and the principal had personally selected and hired naturally had shared characteristics; they were teachers who had chosen to work in a school with a mission of social action and civic engagement, so she assumed they must also be naturally engaged with the world and its issues, informed on a daily basis by reading and listening to the news, and ready to tackle thorny issues as they arose through student questions and conversations.

But after the election of 2016, when the pace of "thorny issues" in the news became fast and furious, Gavrin realized that the assumptions she had made were both erroneous and dangerous. Staff members did not all access up-to-date news regularly, both as a result of limited access (one humanities teacher mentioned the high cost of a daily newspaper subscription) and as a result of busy lives and other personal choices about free time spent differently.

Many shied away from student conversations about the issues of the day, even when they were happening in teachers' presence and even when students' statements about them involved overheard errors, rumors of "fake news," and ideas that offended and disturbed their classmates. Some of the male teachers felt uncomfortable discussing issues of sexism or sexual harassment, and many of the white teachers felt they didn't have the language to discuss race with their African American and Latinx students. While some teachers deftly initiated and led these discussions in their rooms, other just did not know what to say.

Students frequently look to their teachers for guidance, and they raise issues they hear about outside of school to see where the teachers they know and trust stand. A carelessly uttered response or an ill-informed explanation can damage a student's trust or feeling of safety, but a thoughtful conversation with a trusted adult can reassure a student and encourage him to ask, think, and learn more.

Gavrin decided that teachers needed information and practice, and they needed time and space to do so as human beings, not immediately as educators preparing for lessons. Several times over the course of the 2017–2018 school year, she set aside time in faculty meetings for "courageous conversations," borrowing the guidance and language of Glenn Singleton and Curtis Linton's work.

The first was a learning session and discussion, with shared text and video, of the events in Charlottesville, Virginia, in August of 2017; the second was a discussion of #MeToo and sexual harassment in the workplace; and the third happened in the wake of the Parkland, Florida, school shooting. The role of facilitator was a shared responsibility; Gavrin asked teachers to facilitate on two occasions, and for the #MeToo discussion, Gavrin co-facilitated with the school principal (both in an effort to make a strong statement about where the school leaders stood on the issue and to co-facilitate across race and gender).

These conversations are not easy. Nor do they provide instant results. Teachers most often walk away still wrestling with the difficult issues. Sometimes they walk away wrestling with something they heard a colleague say that discomfited them. But the point is that they *wrestled*—that they could not dismiss the issues as something they hadn't heard about, didn't want to talk about, or couldn't tackle.

Teachers tell Gavrin that sometimes they read more after one of these conversations, or they ask directly for help finding more resources. When students approach them about these issues after they have had a chance to begin to process with colleagues, they are at a minimum armed with some baseline information, some resources to share, a desire to learn more along with their students, and the ability to also point the students in the direction of other staff members who may have deeper knowledge talking about the topic.

CONCLUSION

Once, early in her career, someone asked Gavrin what she does for a living and she explained that she was a teacher; the person responded, "I could never be a teacher—I could never do the same thing every day, year after year."

Teaching anywhere, and especially in an urban school, is *never* the same, two days in a row or two years in a row. Teachers have to respond to myriad shifting conditions daily: students' moods and personal needs. The outside experiences the students had the night before that are affecting their readiness to learn that morning.

The conditions they're living in. The conditions of the building, the classroom, and the technology and supplies. The requirements imposed by the school leaders, district leaders, and state education department. The competition for attention with students' ubiquitous cell phones. The issues in the country and the world that demand our attention as well.

To do so, teachers need to be well educated, smart, creative, wise, seasoned professionals. They need to love the work, and they need to stay in the work over time. Building leaders and school systems have a duty to create the conditions for outstanding teachers to thrive.

REFLECTIVE QUESTIONS FOR LEADING IN THE BELLY OF THE BEAST

1. In what ways, or in which elements of their work, are the educators in your school encouraged to think creatively and critically? Where might additional opportunities exist, and how could those be utilized further?

2. Does risk-taking (within the context of teaching and working with students) feel safe and encouraged in your school? If so, how has that climate been constructed and supported? If not, what needs to change?

3. Think about the varied needs of the educators in your school, based on their years of experience and different strengths and weaknesses. How does professional development currently meet those needs? In what ways might the structures and content of professional development change in order to meet them better?

4. Think of a time when controversial or difficult events or issues entered the school community, either directly or through student questions and conversation. What was challenging about that moment? In what ways were the adults prepared to address those issues with students? What space, time, or support were provided for adults to confer with one another about the ways they needed to address the events or issues with students?

5. What else can your school do to encourage you to stretch, grow, and thrive as an educator—to better support you to do the challenging daily work for your students, year after year? How can you take action to help make that happen?

NOTES

1. http://blogs.edweek.org/teachers/classroom_qa_with_larry_ferlazzo/2015/05/response_teachers_stay_because_they_made_a_choice_to_serve.html.

2. https://www.washingtonpost.com/news/answer-sheet/wp/2015/06/12/why-so-many-teachers-leave-and-how-to-get-them-to-stay/?noredirect=on&utm_term=.1c 027ba43d00.

3. https://www.gallup.com/education/237275/why-best-teachers-leaving-ways -keep.aspx.

4. Samantha Leska, Interview. May 23, 2019.

5. https://www.washingtonpost.com/news/answer-sheet/wp/2013/11/30/teacher -slams-scripted-common-core-lessons-that-must-be-taught-word-for-word/?utm_ term=.44f00baded3a.

6. https://www.ajc.com/blog/get-schooled/defeated-too-many-students-and-script ed-instruction-good-teacher-becomes-teacher/gKZrT406yvwzKLvoM7xLEI/.

7. Marco Cenabre, personal communication, April 16, 2018.

8. https://www.gallup.com/education/237275/why-best-teachers-leaving-ways -keep.aspx.

9. A Randomized Controlled Trial of Professional Development for Inter- disciplinary Civic Education: Impacts on Humanities Teachers and Their Students by Dennis J. Barr, Beth Boulay, Robert L. Selman, Rachel McCormick, Ethan Lowenstein, Beth Gamse, Melinda Fine & M. Brielle Leonard—2015.

Chapter 5

Students in the Center

Eran DeSilva

Inclusion is not bringing people into what already exists, it is making a
new space, a better space for everyone.

—George Dei

INTRODUCTION

Growing up as a student of color in a primarily white, affluent high school has
deeply impacted the work of Eran DeSilva as an educator. She was acutely
aware of her differences of being brown, an immigrant, and from a single-
parent family. But she had no space to talk about the feelings or experiences,
and even if she did, she didn't have the words to articulate them. She had no
teachers of color to look to and her white teachers were not facilitating those
conversations in class. In school, she was reading *A Separate Peace* and
Heart of Darkness.

She was studying Greek Civilizations and the Industrial Revolution. She
was one of the editors of a newspaper that usually focused on fashion, sports,
and music. All the while in her head she was wondering why she could never
fully fit in and she loathed her dark skin that kept her from ever being one of
the popular cheerleaders.

DeSilva now works at a private, all-girls school that is much different from
where she went to school. Among the student body, the religious, ethnic,
racial, and socioeconomic diversity is representative of the county in which it
is situated. There is no dominant racial or ethnic group. However, the faculty
and staff demographic are homogenous, 85 percent white and the rest a mix
of other races.

She is proud of the work of her school. It celebrates diversity in its mission and hallmarks, it has student cultural clubs, it encourages interfaith dialogue, it is intentional about keeping a diverse student body, it holds solidarity as one of its core curricular values, and its graduation outcomes include being culturally fluent and respecting differences.

Chasmi was a Muslim student attending this Catholic school. In many ways, she was the "evidence" that the school was accepting of and a beacon for diversity. Her mere presence was a visible indicator of the diversity and perceived safety on campus. She had strong grades, was in honors classes and was thriving. However, Chasmi confessed to her teachers during a student panel about identity in the classroom, that being Muslim at a Catholic school, was not easy. She did not always feel she could be her full self at school or at home.

Her parents did not understand the values of co-curricular or social opportunities in an education program—which meant that she couldn't go to dances or sleepovers, which are parts of the American school experience. Consequently, there were limits to her sense of belonging because she was not able to participate in some meaningful social experiences. Moreover, she did not always feel like she could fully express her religious beliefs at school because though it valued diversity, Islam had some fundamental differences that she did not always have the skill set to bridge.

Chasmi did not have a place to genuinely discuss what she was experiencing and her teachers did not know that she needed that space. Indicators such as grades, friendships, and college acceptance, pointed to a successful education. But the internal process and challenges were not so readily apparent. It was not enough to merely have Muslim students or students of color on campus, this only achieves representational diversity.

To truly reach inclusion where all students are seen and heard, much deeper work must be done. "Rather than focus on the visible "fruits" of culture—dress, food, holidays, and heroes—we have to focus on the roots of culture: worldview, core beliefs, and group values" (Hammond 2014, 25).

Educators often have good intentions and noble goals that inspire their work with students and drive decision-making. But good intentions are not enough when striving for full inclusion and realizing equity. The lived reality of diversity is much more complicated, nuanced, and gritty than these articulated ideals of "embracing diversity." To truly live and work with young people who come from a diverse set of backgrounds, experiences, and identities, educators need to have the ability to navigate conversations and experiences about identity, diversity, and inclusion. Students need to be fully seen and understood in order to make thoughtful decisions as well as align practices with equity and inclusion.

School leaders need to listen to student voices, provide space for meaningful dialogue around issues, and build a community of support among staff and students. This is a daunting task. But a critical move for school leaders is to bring students to the conversation in order to combat implicit bias and deepen understanding of diverse perspectives and experiences that exist in the school community.

It is imperative that school leaders take the time to develop trusting and authentic relationships with students in order to fully understand the impact of school instruction, policies, and assessment. Once these relationships are established, a leader can truly value and harness the power, creativity, skills, and experiences of students to support the school's commitment to inclusion, equity, and just decision-making.

As the director of Professional Development, Eran DeSilva is responsible for supporting teacher growth, keeping up with current educational research, and working with other school leaders in ensuring that the practices and policies are meeting the needs of students. In her first years in this position, she launched a strand of professional development called Identity, Diversity, and Inclusion. She held a series of workshops that explored how identity impacts the work of both students and educators.

It was a new program for the school designed to intentionally discuss and understand how the diverse student body could be a safe and inclusive space for everyone. Faculty and staff did come to some new shared understandings, but the work felt detached from the everyday decisions that are made in the classrooms and meetings.

Five years into her work, DeSilva realized that the discussion on inclusion and equity could not be isolated in its own strand of learning because identity and equity were intertwined in all parts of educational policy and practice either explicitly or implicitly. However, it was difficult to articulate that when a colorblind approach is deeply embedded into the education system. All students are seen as "equal" and treated "the same," without acknowledging differences and then adapting practice to meet the variety of needs and experiences. The reality is that schools in America are deeply rooted in a historical legacy of sorting and identifying students according "ability" or markers such as race, gender, ability, and class.

Therefore, educators who are truly committed to transforming schools need to address how to meet student populations with growing diversity. From issues of grading to classroom culture, students can help educators to understand how identity permeates all issues. School leaders need to find ways to bring student voice to professional development and policy-making. A school leader can do this by 1) cultivating authentic, trusting relationships with students to understand the daily impact of school policies, 2) provide space for meaningful dialogue between faculty and students, and 3) promoting a learner mindset and cultural humility among the faculty, staff, and administrators on school sites.

WHAT IS THE VALUE OF STUDENT VOICE
WHEN CREATING SCHOOL POLICY?

A leader has an endless list of demands on her time and energy. It is easy to become focused only on administrative tasks or the management of the school. Although these are necessary pieces for the day-to-day operations of the school, it does not necessarily allow for the daily commitment to empowering teachers and students to become their best selves. In order to make sure that the fundamental purpose of schools—helping students realize their full potential—is happening, leaders need to have a direct line to students. That connection allows leaders to look beyond the data, and hear the personal stories of the learning, growth, and struggle.

Besides the focus of instruction, the key focus of education is assessment and reporting of grades. It can be the gatekeeper into higher education that allows or obstructs students from reaching their full academic potential. Recent research has examined the role of grading and assessment in bridging the achievement gap and reaching true equity in schools. Joe Feldman documents how current grading practices and procedures are biased, inaccurate, and undermining true student learning in his book *Grading for Equity: What It Is, Why It Matters, and How It Can Transform Schools and Classrooms.*

Feldman traces the history of grading practices explaining that the traditional grading practices of assigning A–F letter grades emerged as a need to produce a standardized reporting of student ability and achievement in the early 1900s. This grading system "exists almost unchanged today: Students receive a letter grade in each class that represents their performance. In many classrooms, those grades are assigned with the normal curve in mind, and these grades are used to sort students into different tracks and opportunities" (Feldman 2019, 24). Yet most schools continue to use this outdated system, even though riddled with flaws and inconsistencies.

The shift to standards-based grading supports current understanding of cognitive flexibility, growth mindset, and equity in grading. Yet, teachers tend to be very resistant to changing this paradigm of assessment.

> Because each teacher's grading system is virtually unregulated and unconstrained, a teacher's grading policies and practices reveal how she defines and envisions her relationship to students, what she predicts best prepares them for success, her beliefs about students, and her self-concept as a teacher. That's why challenges to our grading practices don't just offend our professional judgement; they can invoke an emotional and psychological threat. (Feldman 2019, 6)

School leaders are met with resistance to changing grading practices and structures in even the most progressive faculties.

When DeSilva, as the director of Professional Development and a member of the instructional leadership team, worked with her Vice Principal on reforming grading and assessment practices at her school, they were faced with skepticism and reluctance. It was very difficult to bring teachers into the discussion without a sense of defensiveness because it called into question the validity of what all of the teachers, including DeSilva, had been doing for their entire career. It was difficult to confront the idea that the policies and procedures they had been using for decades were not only inequitable but also potential harmful to students. As Feldman writes,

> Most of us entered teaching to build meaningful relationships with young people, to engender in them a sense of trust and safety by accepting mistakes along a path to proficiency, but our traditional grading encourages us to judge nearly everything a student does or doesn't do, and we create pressure-cooker classrooms where no mistake goes unpenalized. Effective teacher-student relationships require students' confidence that the classroom is a space to take risks without penalty, to disclose weaknesses without being judged, to simply feel safe knowing that they don't have to perform perfectly day in and day out. Our traditional practice of grading *everything* students do inadvertently creates a distrust, shame, and deceit—undermining the teacher-student relationship qualities that support learning. (Feldman 2019, 32)

How could DeSilva and her Vice Principal change the hearts and minds of the teachers and of their collective thinking? It seemed like a daunting and impossible task. Teachers felt that students were well supported and thriving in the current system. Ninety-nine percent of their students continued to college after graduating. What would convince and motivate teachers to change the deeply held beliefs about current grading and assessment?

And then in the midst of the process, DeSilva found an email in her inbox from Cynthia a junior in her AP US History class entitled "A Letter to Educators." It was an open letter that her student wanted shared at the last faculty meeting of the year. It addressed a variety of school issues, including grades, from a student perspective.

> We need to stop perpetuating this toxic mentality that the only means to life and career success is through a 36, a 1600, a 5, a 100, or an A. In my own years of schooling, one thing I have noticed is the shared sentiment that when students do not do well in a class, it is because they are not trying hard enough. I have to make this point very clear right now because I have experienced this judgement and faced assumption after assumption for so long on this basis.
>
> I have to pull from an example of my own this year in which I took a test, for which I studied for two weeks. I was out of town during the original administering

of this test and took my textbook with me on a trip to an International Science Conference to study. There are rain stains on my book as proof of this. When I came back to take the test, I was suddenly overwhelmed with the realization of what weight this test had on my semester grade in a class with few entered scores.

I knew that material like the back of my hand, yet when I got to the testing room, I froze halfway through the test in an absolute state of panic. The time was ticking, I had only gotten halfway through and the only thought occupying my mind was the grade I would get on this test. I never wrote anything for the other half of the test. I couldn't move my hands.

When I explained this to my teacher later, I was told that it was clear I had a panic episode and that this was unusual of me, but I would not be allowed to do corrections because our class had already been given "enough opportunities" to fix our grades. I received a 50% on that test, a test I finished half of.

So there I am, a broken shell of a human being in front of my teacher, drained of all confidence in an environment that values me primarily for my academic contributions, only to be told with a pat on the shoulder that I'll get a better grade next semester if I try harder. If we are to say that school should be about learning and not grades, why does no one actually believe so or act in such a way that promotes this mentality.

Grades and effort are not entirely correlated. It is not fair to assume that we are just kids and have no reason to be stressed. It is not fair to assume that every time we mention a family emergency that it is just some cheap excuse to get out of classwork.

Here, on paper, from the mind and heart of a young person who the school was committed to listen to and value, was the impact of the grading practices. It was not the theoretical framework or statistical data. It was the very real and tangible lived experience of a student who sat in DeSilva's class week after week. Despite her best efforts to create a supportive assessment policy of retakes and no late work penalty, there was still a larger context of grading policy that had day-to-day implications on her student's health, well-being, and success.

One of the issues that this junior raised was the assumption that teachers make about student behavior and intentions when she said, "It is not fair to assume that every time we mention a family emergency, that it is just some cheap excuse to get out of classwork." It is important for all teachers to recognize that there is implicit bias in the work and assessment of student performance. What "effort," "hard work," or "participation" looks and feels like depends on culture and family values. Therefore, it is hard to objectively quantify or make judgments about how hard a student is trying or how much time is reasonable for test preparation given the diversity of students in the classroom.

Feldman overlays the concept of implicit bias to grading practices and writes, "When we observe someone, we bring to that observation a set of assumptions and beliefs that color our interpretation of that person's action. Most of the time those assumptions are subconscious and ingrained in us at an early age, a phenomenon called 'implicit bias.' No one is immune to implicit biases'. . . . Teachers' implicit biases and subjective interpretations of students' behaviors influence how teachers respond in terms of both discipline and instruction" (Feldman 2019, 42). In her letter, Cynthia identifies how this bias shows up in a daily way.

Authentically listening to students enables educators to understand the impact of school culture and policies about instruction, assessment, grading, and discipline. Including student voice is powerful and can be a call to do the hard work required for radical transformation of our schools. And students want to be part of the solution. Cynthia continues in her "Letter to Educators":

> I've been a student for most of my life. For over thirteen years, I have walked in and out of buildings where I spend my hours from eight in the morning until almost 6 pm (not uncommon for those with working parents, or in my case singular). That comes out to nearly 23,000 hours of my life that I have spent in educational institutions, and I am ashamed that it has taken me this long to build up the courage to give my two cents on the flaws of our education system.

> I don't mean this in regards to our school alone, but to our society as a whole. Sure, we discuss the injustices of the education system in our classes but we tend to distance it from the notion that some of those flaws may run deep through our own hallways and plague our own classrooms. I should have said these things a long time ago, but for too long I have been afraid of facing authority.

> I regret not speaking up earlier about the flaws that I noticed in my own schools because every class that has come after me has faced the same things and still no one is bold enough to say anything. I'm making an active choice to break that silence right now and say something.

> I must start this off with the realization that in every meeting about improving the education system internally, *I have never seen an actual student present. It baffles me that in a discussion about the best interests of the students, there are no physical students to voice their comments and concerns.* School is not a

one-sided ordeal; it's a cohesive learning experience for both the teachers and students involved, so why is it that only the teachers are in the room when conversations are held about the necessary change in our curriculum.

We are taught to not be bystanders but that is exactly what we are in this situation. We are allowing these stress levels to continue on the rise, we are supporting the monopoly and industrialization of education, we are being complacent with the fact that the education system is losing its purpose and derailing from its mission statement in a way that is going to be destructive to both the educators and students involved.

School leaders such as DeSilva need to recognize the value of student voice in the reimagining of education. There needs to be time and space dedicated to sharing and honoring student stories. Young people can help their teachers learn about inclusion, equity, justice, identity, and compassion. They only need to be given the opportunity. It will require the adults on campus to do deep reflection, interrogate their practices with honesty, and have difficult conversations with their colleagues. But teachers who are committed to their students fully realizing their potential and becoming their best selves will undoubtedly be up for the challenge.

This email asks, or perhaps demands, including students in decision-making. Students are a valuable and underutilized resource in teacher growth and school decision-making. They are at the center of the work of educators—the motivation for endless hours of work, the driver of our instructional decisions, and the final "product" of schools. And yet, students' voices are often not at the table when it comes to critical conversations about student learning, well-being, and success. School leaders must learn to value and leverage student experiences and skills. This means giving them power and permission to lead and teach rather than listen and learn.

CULTIVATING AUTHENTIC RELATIONSHIPS

DeSilva asked Cynthia why she sent this impassioned and candid email to her. The junior responded, "Because I know you care. I see how you are in class and trust you." This relationship took time and effort to cultivate, the daily interaction between a teacher and a student. The demands on a school leader are endless, the hours that leadership requires are long—but having direct contact with students is imperative. Direct contact means having the space and opportunity to work closely with students on a regular basis. This is critical because it takes time to cultivate relationships, trusting and deep relationships with students.

In her work as a school leader, DeSilva knows how important it is to stay close and connected to the students she serves. DeSilva teaches at least one course per semester, has an advisory group, and is moderator for a student leadership group. Each of these spaces allow for different types of interactions and meaningful engagement with students. And in each setting, she intentionally listens to and learns from students.

This is particularly important for students of color, who often need more outreach and invitation to engage in school decisions and practices. Her fellow teacher leaders have said that staying in the classroom splits her time and focus away from administrative responsibilities that are great and growing. However, staying in the classroom is a nonnegotiable for her. Why prioritize this work with students when the demands of a school leader are so great?

DeSilva knows she needs students to trust her if she wants to have the hard conversations about equity and inclusion with them. It takes time and intention to grow a trusting relationship with students. The daily interaction with students lays the foundation to have the difficult conversations. This type of relationship cannot be achieved by the occasional coffee with the principal or walking through the hallways during lunch. School leaders need the type of relationship that allows for a candid and honest dialogue requires intention, time, attention, and effort. A school leadership team should find ways to support each other in creating this opportunity for this type of direct service with students to occur. By having this genuine connection with students, leaders are able to discover the true impact of school policies and practices have on students.

STUDENT CONVERSATIONS ABOUT DIVERSITY

DeSilva works with a group of student leaders weekly to discuss issues of social justice. These leaders generated a proposal for the creation of a Diversity Council, a group where presidents of each affinity club (such as the Black Student Union, Alliance, Muslim Student Association) would come together to talk about issues, experiences, and events. Over time, the members representing different groups came together and created the following mission statement:

> We the Diversity Council work collectively to strengthen our sense of pride and community at Notre Dame while recognizing and celebrating our differences. We strive to educate our community about our unique identities, cultures, and experiences. We seek to foster a sense of respect and appreciation for diversity as we empower one another. We stand in solidarity to collaborate and advocate for equity, justice, and inclusion.

The Diversity Council would create a space for dialogue between diverse students and recognize the intersectionality between them. DeSilva thought it was a beautiful and courageous idea that would bring students who feel marginalized together to share their stories and give them agency. It would provide a space for them to do collective thinking and become advocates for issues that impacted them. It had powerful potential.

As she explained the concept and efforts of the students, her colleague listened patiently. She then said, cautiously, "Well, I know I can say this to you without you taking it the wrong way, but . . . we need to be careful because our white students will feel left out. Where do our white students get this type of space?" Here was a fear of upsetting white students, which in turn limited the potential of students of color to build solidarity and community among one another. This moment challenged the very essence of embracing diversity.

DeSilva was at a loss for words. She felt a mix of emotions surge through her—thankful that this person was so comfortable to share such an honest opinion so candidly and deeply unsettled that one of her administrators had such an ill-informed, underdeveloped understanding of race that was rooted in colorblindness. Regretfully, she did not share any of these emotions or have the courage to lead the real conversation necessary at that moment. Instead, she left her office feeling dejected and disillusioned. How could the school truly live its mission of inclusion if the adults weren't having honest conversations about race? And how was it that the students were doing complicated work on intersectionality while adults did not see its value?

Students hold incredible capacity and potential for navigating the current explosive racial crisis America faces. DeSilva witnesses this every year when she teaches her Race, Identity, and Community unit in her Contemporary Social Issues course. To set the stage and norms for the conversation, she asks seniors "Why is it hard to talk about race?" Hands shoot up and they eagerly share their opinions: *It's uncomfortable. It's taboo. You are afraid of offending someone. You are afraid of being hurt. You might say something racist. I might have to call someone else out for being racist.* They unabashedly share their feelings with their peers and with their teacher before diving into the study of race in America.

A few weeks later, she asks the same question of her faculty, "Why is it hard to talk about race?" The quiet discomfort is palpable. It is difficult being one of five teachers of color in the room. Why was the conversation about race and identity so much easier to have with students? Why were students more willing to lean in and tackle the hard topics? Why were her student leaders recognizing intersectionality and developing space for this on her campus? DeSilva is self-conscious of her brown skin, much like she was as a high school student. It makes her the outsider who does not quite fit in with the rest of the group.

Each day she enjoys collaborating with her colleagues, but there are moments when her identity creates tension and isolation. Being one of a few educators of color, there are moments when her experiences and perspectives are divergent from the white majority. She is afraid to "talk about race again" because it makes her mostly white staff uncomfortable. Students possess a skill set, willingness, and courage to engage in this hard work that adults sometimes shy away from.

DIALOGING AND LEARNING FROM STUDENTS

DeSilva decided to have a student panel that would share their experiences from class with the faculty. They would bring the difficult content to their teachers and challenge the teachers to grapple with the complexities of gender, race, and identity. It would also showcase critical thinking and communication skills to dialogue about hard topics as well as the lived experiences of diversity that are not observable on tests or projects. DeSilva witnessed these skills and voices shining in her classroom every day, realizing how much potential they had to teach her faculty.

One of the students on the panel was an African American senior. Tamara is the daughter of a Nigerian father and an African American mother who grew up in the South. In her social studies classes she often felt the burden of being the only black student in class who implicitly or explicitly became "the voice" for minorities in general and of the "black voice" specifically during discussions deconstructing *Huck Finn* or exploring the emergence of Black Lives Matter.

She spoke of the heavy burden, as well as how it limited her ability to be angry and express her true, raw emotion. She held back in situations because she didn't want to be labeled as an "angry black woman."

Teachers had respect for Tamara but her outgoing, outspoken personality covered up the frustration she felt. They were surprised to hear that she struggled with being "the voice" for black students. Tamara spoke eloquently and powerfully about her own identity and understanding of race. She possessed insights that only a young black woman could. She felt the impact of implicit bias and racial dynamics that were playing out in the classroom because of the color of her skin. There was no intention to marginalize her, but the space was not safe for her to use her full voice.

Tamara's teachers were well intentioned, compassionate, and caring. They were surprised to hear that she felt singled out because they had never intentionally done this. How was it that this could have occurred? And why was race such a salient issue for Tamara in the classroom? Beverly Tatem's foundational work, *Why are all the black kids sitting together in the cafeteria?* explores the process of racialization and development in children through young adulthood.

She asks,

> Why do Black youths, in particular think about themselves in terms of race? Because that is how the rest of the world thinks of them. Our self-perceptions are shaped by the messages that we receive from those around us, and when young Black men and women enter adolescence, the racial content of those messages intensifies. (Tatem 2003, 53–54)

Research shows that racial identity development is a critical part of adolescence and school experience, particularly for students of color. Tatem continues,

> "A study of Black and White eighth graders from an integrated urban junior high school, Jean Phinney and Steve Traver found clear evidence for the beginning of the search process in this dimension of identity. Among forty-eight participants, more than a third had thought about the effects of ethnicity on their future, had discussed issues with family and friends and were attempting to learn more about their group. While white students in this integrated school were also beginning to think about ethnic identity, there was evidence to suggest a more active search among Black students, especially Black females. Phinney and Tarver's research is consistent with my own study of Black youth in predominantly White communities, where the environmental cues that trigger an examination of racial identity often become evident in middle school or junior high school." (2003, 55–56)

Tamara had been developing her black racial identity even before coming to high school. The experience of being only one of five black students at the school made it difficult for her to find others with whom to share her journey. Tatem helps to explain Tamara's personal narrative stating, "Resisting the stereotypes and affirming other definitions of themselves is part of the task facing young Black women in both White and Black communities" (57).

Good intentions and kindness are not enough when it comes to helping students like Tamara to fully reach their potential and explore the complicated issues of identity development. These intentions do not erase the harmful impact that colorblind strategies and approaches have on students. Educators need to acknowledge that students of diverse backgrounds are having very unique and different experiences in the same classroom.

There needs to be an interrogation of the "universalism" that

assumes that whites and people of color have the same realities, the same experiences in the same contexts (i.e., I feel comfortable in this majority white classroom, so you must too), the same response from others, and assumes that the same doors are open to all. Acknowledging racism as a system of privilege conferred on whites challenges claims to universalism. (DiAngelo 2011, 59)

This acknowledgement can confront the colorblind framework that permeates school practices. Students can be partners in this work.

For education to be truly transformative and liberatory in an inequitable school system, professional development has to include students in a new way. It is important to look beyond the traditional canon of curriculum and professional development venues to find valuable teacher education. As Bettina Love critically examines an oppressive, inequitable education system, she proposes "Pedagogy should work in tandem with students' own knowledge of their community and grassroots organizations to push forward new ideas for social change, not just to be a tool to enhance test scores or grades" (Love 2019, 19).

School leaders need to honor that youth bring a wealth of knowledge, experience, and insight to the table. They have *experienced* the education system as users and recipients of policies. Therefore, their voice is valuable. DeSilva recognizes this in big and small ways because she is open and listening to students all the time. Moreover, she seeks to partner with them in the work for a more just society.

Recently she worked with two ambitious and inspiring young people and students, Winona Guo and Priya Vulchi. The two embarked on a journey to explore the impact of race on individual and collective identity in the United States. Their goal was to create a resource to help develop racial literacy in classrooms. They chose to take a gap year to interview individuals from every state and compile the experiences into a book called *Tell Me Who You Are: Sharing Our Stories of Race, Culture, and Identity*. DeSilva was part of their editing team and now a member of the educator advisory board piloting curriculum.

She values the lessons that Winona and Priya have to offer her and appreciates that the two push her to broaden her own racial consciousness and understanding in ways that she could never imagine. These two young people display courage and insights that many adults have not yet realized. They write in the introduction of their book,

Any person who is part of a community can help ensure that the voices within that community are heard. We can prevent some of our racial pain before it seeps into our younger generations. We can heal the communities we are already part of so they are defined not by division but by hope and harmony, by love, and equity. If we can do it, why don't we? The truth of the world—that race is inextricable with everyday life—is heavy. But if we all cared and dared to share the weight of that truth, perhaps we can hold it high enough and long enough for things to change. Perhaps if we start by simply recognizing that race impacts everything, that everything is impacted by race, our vision would begin to clear. (Guo and Vulchi 2019)

The bravery, hope, and honesty that Winona and Priya have are ideals that all educators should strive for in their practice. It is what allows for a true interrogation of current practices in order to align our actions with the lofty goals of inclusion and equity. Students can inform educators of the impact of instructional decisions and policies through their lived experience and unique perspectives that inform.

CULTURAL HUMILITY

Only by taking a learner stance, will educators have the humility needed to do the true work of equity. A learner knows that there is never one answer and there is always more to discover. In *The Principal's Companion: Strategies to Lead Schools to Student and Teacher Success*, Pam Robbins and Harvey Alvy say, "the leader can model for everyone in the workplace what lifelong learning means. For modeling to be effective, though, it should be sincere, consistent, purposeful, and empowering" (Robbins and Alvy 2014, 3).

This approach is critical if educators are to honestly confront implicit bias and build cultural competency. It allows educators to have cultural humility because they are allowed to not know all the answers and push the boundaries of their own thinking and understanding.

As Jim Knight, education leader and coaching expert, writes in *Unmistakable Impact*, "Humility also means that we are more concerned with getting things right rather than being right. Therefore, we ask good questions, questions to which we don't know the answers, and we listen for answers. We stop trying to persuade and start trying to learn" (Knight 2010, 39). Understanding the importance of humility, DeSilva seeks to constantly engage in dialogue with teachers and students in an effort to understand and learn from them.

DeSilva knew from her own experience as a student that identity influenced her experiences in school. However, educators who are using a colorblind framework may not be able to recognize and honor the way identity shapes the work of educators and students. Educators must approach diverse learning communities with cultural humility rather than cultural competence. To be culturally competent means that there is an endpoint to learning and understanding. It translates to achieving an outcome, rather than being open to continually learning and recognizing implicit bias.

Melanie Tervalon and Jann Murray-Garcia compare the approach of cultural humility versus cultural competence in their work as physicians. The two women propose that "Cultural humility incorporates a lifelong commitment to self-evaluation and self-critique, to redressing the power imbalances in the patient-physician dynamic, and to developing mutually beneficial and nonpaternalistic clinical and advocacy partnerships with communities on behalf of individuals and defined populations" (Tervalon and Garcia 1998, 117).

Much like educators, doctors are in positions of power that influence the well-being and growth of their patients. Approaching students, parents, and colleagues with cultural humility, opens up the possibility for open dialogue and deeper understanding across diverse communities. And by doing so, ensures that their practices meet the needs of those they serve.

During a student panel, Lilian shared her experiences as a first-generation student from a family that had fled the Vietnam War and sought refuge in the United States. She was a strong student, in accelerated classes, involved in student leadership, and well liked by her teachers and peers. But what few teachers knew was that Lilian was living in two worlds with two different realities. There was conflict between her home and school values because she was growing up bicultural. Her school community valued speaking up and using your voice. Her home saw obedience as a sign of respect. So while her teachers encouraged her to question and push back on ideas, her parents expected her to follow rules and comply to the norm.

Lilian talked about how this was confusing and challenging. Also, the social norms went beyond behavior and into beliefs. She learned about gender fluidity and transgender issues in DeSilva's class, while her parents were traditional Catholics who were not readily embracing the justice issues of the LGBTQ community. She shared how navigating this dual reality was heartbreaking at times.

Where did Lilian seek support as her school and home contexts collided? She was able to navigate and bridge these realities because of her mentor in advisory, Ms. Nguyen. Her mentor was a Vietnamese immigrant who knew Lilian's story personally as well as professionally. The identity of the teacher was the critical component because Ms. Nguyen could truly hear, empathize, and then support Lilian. She could hold the space for that kind of conversation to take place. Identity mattered.

Lilian's experiences illustrate the complicated, layered identity of some students. She was first generation, an immigrant, a female, and a student of color. Understanding the nuances of her personal identity and development is complicated. Kimberle Crenshaw coined the term *intersectionality* in her groundbreaking essay, "Demarginalizing the Intersection of Race and Sex: A Black Feminist Critique of Antidiscrimination Doctrine, Feminist Theory and Antiracist Politics" in 1989.

In an interview celebrating the African American Policy Forum in 2017, Crenshaw explained that "Intersectionality is a lens through which you can see where power comes and collides, where it interlocks and intersects. It's not simply that there's a race problem here, a gender problem here, and a class or LBGTQ problem there. Many times that framework erases what happens to people who are subject to all of these things" ("Kimberlé Crenshaw on Intersectionality, More than Two Decades Later" Colombia Law School).

Lilian lived intersectionality in her day-to-day high school experience. Teachers of color such as DeSilva and Nguyen can often empathize with her experience because of their own identity and personal journey. But all teachers must use the "prism" of intersectionality to truly serve their diverse student body because with "no name for a problem, you can't see a problem . . . and you can't solve it" (Crenshaw Ted Talk "The Urgency of Intersectionality" 2016).

Lilian's challenge was that she was navigating different worlds and code switching between them, without the space to discuss it. Much like Tamara, she had to figure out how to bridge two worlds, conflicting norms, and incongruent values in isolation. Until asked to speak to the faculty, she never reflected and articulated her own intersectional experience.

Students like Lilian need teachers who see their full, layered identity. But this requires internal work on the part of teachers. Zaretta Hammond's work on culturally responsive teaching seeks to equip teachers to work with diverse backgrounds effectively and thoughtfully. In her book *Culturally Responsive Teaching and the Brain: Promoting Authentic Engagement and Rigor among Culturally and Linguistically Diverse Students*, she shares,

> Being responsive to diverse students' needs asks teachers to be mindful and present. That requires reflection. Engaging in reflection helps culturally responsive teachers recognize the beliefs, behaviors, and practices that get in the way of their ability to respond constructively and positively to students. The true power of culturally responsive teaching comes from being comfortable in your own skin because you are not a neutral party in the process. You can never take yourself out of the equation. Instead you must commit to the journey. This means we each must do the "inside-out" work required: developing the right

mindset, engaging in self reflection, checking our implicit biases, practicing social-emotional awareness, and holding an inquiry stance regarding the impact of our interactions on students. (Hammond 2014, 53)

Hammond is explicit in naming how difficult and deep the work is when striving to truly create an inclusive learning environment for diverse student bodies. It requires commitment to do not only an interrogation of professional practice, but also an internal reflection on identity and beliefs. School leaders need to make the time and provide the support for teachers to truly see and understand the layers and complexity to student identity. Lilian provided the call to action. With cultural humility, school leaders and educators remain open and promote dialogue with students to promote full inclusion and grow collective understanding of diversity.

CONCLUSION

DeSilva believes as a school leader that she has to commit to lifelong learning and humility. She never settles for one answer and seeks a broad range of perspectives, knowing that the experience of school is not uniform. Each student experiences school in the same buildings on the same campus in very different and sometimes divergent ways. There is no "one size fits all" or "universal education approach." Our schools are becoming increasingly diverse in a country that proclaims its ideas are justice, equity, and democracy.

For all students to truly have access to a meaningful education and reach their full potential, educators and school leaders need to truly listen to them and see their complex identities. To do so, school leaders need to prioritize these direct interactions with students and cultivate trusting relationships with them so that they can be honest about their school experiences. By doing so, they create a space for students and teachers to partner in the work for justice and inclusion.

REFLECTIVE QUESTIONS FOR LEADING
IN THE BELLY OF THE BEAST

1. What opportunities do you create for students to share their perspectives and experiences with faculty and administration in an authentic and honest way? How do you communicate to students that their voices are genuinely honored and valued?
2. What systems and structures are in place at your school to ensure that student voice and experience have an authentic impact of decisions that are made?

3. What are ways in which you ensure diverse voices are able to share in a safe and inclusive environment? What are obstacles to this type of sharing and dialogue? How do you navigate these obstacles?
4. In what ways does cultural humility live in everyday interactions between adults at your site? How do you model it as a leader? Among students? Among different stakeholders?

Chapter 6

"This is the Work"

A Personal and Professional Working for Sustaining in the Belly of the Beast

Timothy Bremner

The question then lies in determining how to turn difficulties into possibility. For that reason, in the struggle for change, we must be neither solely patient nor solely impatient, but patiently impatient. Unlimited patience, that is never restless, ends up immobilizing transformative action. The same is the case with willful impatience, which demands immediate results from action even while it is still being planned . . . . The answer is in the balanced dosage of both patience and impatience. The world cannot be transformed without either one, for both are needed. (Freire 1997, 64)

INTRODUCTION

As educator Timothy Bremner begins to close another year, which is really just ramping up for the next year, he is in a position of having the same conversation with effective teachers who are leaving—trying to remind them, convince them, encourage them to stay. Simultaneously, he is having conversations about how to facilitate the exit of those who are clearly not serving young people at all. Meanwhile he is reaching out, beginning conversations, starting relationships, with new people, most of them brand new to the profession, who are coming to work at one of the most challenging schools in the city. He did this last year. He will do it next year.

For him, there is a through line within all of these conversations, which represents the spectrum of successes and failures of our education system. It is exemplified by the mantra that, for better or worse, has kept him in this system, the game, the belly of the beast, for twenty years. He reminds himself and others, *this is the work.*

Trite. Yes. Cliche. Yes. Simple. Yes. And yet this is what Bremner has come to rely on in some of the most complicated, celebrated, frustrating, backward, and dysfunctional scenarios in his career. Beneath this simple phrase, however, lies deep understandings, necessary assumptions and ultimately a profound stance and approach to education in this country. For him, it is the "patient impatience" Freire identifies as a key to sustaining the strength, commitment, and resilience to show up, survive, and innovate within a system that is designed to fail many in order to benefit a few.

This perspective is not new, and neither is the ongoing struggle to develop and sustain culture, independent learners, quality teaching, and community in schools. From this stance, then, the work is to face the dysfunction that maintains a status quo bred from white supremacy, patriarchy, hyper-capitalism, gender, and other oppressions of intersectionality—and proceed, not with resignation, mediocrity and status quo, but rather with a coal-like burn, slow, hot, and at times in flame in order to remedy the belly and transform the beast.

The work is a reflection on Bremner's own practice, his personal words of advice to keep him sane in the face of insanity and in spite of his complicity. A straight, white, cis-gendered man, not from the communities with whom he works, but of the belief that his own liberation is in partnership with the critical minds that he has the honor to engage with in this work of education, transformation, and future creation.

A simple mantra, but one he continues to reflect and rely on personally and professionally in these moments of contradictory conversations of hiring, firing, moving on, or staying in a system that, for the students of color in deep East Oakland, is ultimately failing. He reminds himself that this is his purpose, to not give in, to continue to push, create, struggle, fail, try again. After all, what is the alternative? This place for him is the cutting edge. Our inspiration and our hope of collective liberation in alliance with our youth who walk in the door every day.

The work is a discussion with a new but very effective, innovative, and passionate teacher who has reached a breaking point with ineffective leadership, dispassionate colleagues, or the racism of low expectations and normalized mediocrity. Bremner reminds them, you are right and this is what we do, to identify, interrupt, build, maintain, and sustain even small pockets of something better, a few healthy relationships, a smile, an engaging lesson for students walking in our doors in the face of all that is backward. That is the point. As contradictory, paradoxically tragic as it is, it is resistance; we must make it transformative, to survive and to thrive. To work in collaboration in order to reckon and to regenerate.

The work includes conversations with new and passionate teachers about the highs and lows of what it means to teach, really teach for more than two years, to face a five-year wall and choose to continue, words that have no grounding without the first-year experience of having shed the tears, shared the laughs, experienced the day-to-day good and bad of classroom teaching.

It is an aligning of reality and perception to hold this stance on a daily basis set against historic marginalization and systems established to see students of color, poor students, and others "on the edge" of a hegemonic culture, fail. It is facing the implications of and response to these conditions on the part of our students and the days ahead that will challenge the very core of their being. He says, "New teacher, you don't really hear me *yet*, but we'll have this conversation again."

In a similar vein, it is a conversation with a critical pedagogue to offer the idea that "and/both" is actually a way forward and to reflect in order to collaborate with colleagues to push and be pushed is how we move systems. "You are right and your ego is strong, your colleagues are needed and may need you whether you want them or not. It's our work to create collective accountability." A reminder that solid best practices that build relationships to grow skills toward students' fullest potential within the context of their lives is as revolutionary as naming systems of oppression and tapping current cultural trends to connect and engage young people.

The work rallies our collective spirit, energy, and skill to carry on even when every logic, sign, and breaking point has been past. Despite all of the failures and systemic oppressions that contradict our own humanity and that of the young people whom we serve, the reliance on each other founded on collective values, meaning making, and directions toward common notions of success is tantamount.

We must know ourselves, find our folks, build co-conspirators, and make a path. As Bettina Love writes, "When pursuing educational freedom—really, all freedoms—survival cannot be the goal, and finding a place somewhere on the spectrum cannot be, either. The goal must be pursuing freedom at all costs as a collective group of abolitionism-minded people who welcome struggle" (Love 2019, 161).

In the end, it is many conversations. It's between school leaders managing yet again the next new initiative, it's with students about the importance of this one assignment and why it really does mean your future: really though. It's between colleagues and friends, and with friends that are colleagues about inspiration, hope, dedication and coming back again. And again. And again. It's what Kristin Botello describes as "tenacious love" in chapter 3. And, more simply, it is Bremner's conversation with himself as he grapples with his own calling, identity, experience, and need for breath mired in systemic dysfunction. And, as he looks at his students, and at his colleagues and it all becomes clear. He hears you. He sees you. And this is the work.

THE WORK: OPIATE OR SPARK?

In writing this chapter, Bremner asks himself: What does he have to say; what has not been said; what is his voice, and what does he have to offer? Especially if his offering is "This is the Work." At first glance, it can be a call to work harder, just do, put up with it and it will get better, complacency and ultimately disempowerment. He offers his experience that consists of his drive, his successes and failures through the "seasons" of what Love calls the "education survival complex" and it's "spirit murder" of black and brown kids (Love 2019). Part of this complex is what Bremner calls The Grind, The Drag, The Churn, the 5 Year Wall, and lastly the 20+ Year Slump.

These are moments in the experience of educators in schools that can be either catalysts or nails in the coffin of quality teaching practice. Similar to death by a thousand cuts, much of the experience for youth and adults in schools chips away at a person's energy, passion, and desire to learn. These are spirit killers for schools as learning organizations and students and adults as people in schools too.

The Grind is the day-to-day, minute-minute responsibility and shuffling of students and assignments through a system modeled from and aspiring to produce products for market. The Drag are those times in mid-fall and later again mid-spring where curriculum and morale fall flat, inspiration is vapid, the weeks long and the days even longer. If you've been there, you know what it means. The Churn is the teacher retention crisis where one to two-year careers are cut short for the passionate but disillusioned and the exploiting career climber that "just decided" to go to Med School.

If one is skilled, lucky, or confused enough to last until year 5, Bremner has found in his own experience and that of others, a *wall* as evidenced by narratives like "perhaps all I've been doing, as much as I love it, is for nothing" or "I've reached an age that maybe it's time to try something else," or "maybe education isn't for me, I'm not feeling as successful or inspired, I should be better at what I do by know" and "I've tried, but I'm not feeling heard or seen at this school."

To weather these "seasons" in one's career is one charge for the transformative teacher and leader. Ideally, a person with the right combination of stance, team, and tools might just survive for another five years; they might just thrive for another twenty and not only avoid becoming an entrenched, bitter cog in the machine, but become an inspirational, co-conspirator working in partnership with youth and community to levy our collective assets and cultural wealth through an intersectional approach in order to innovate a home in school and serve a participatory democracy.

Maybe, with the right perspective and stance, role of transformative leadership in education might become more sustainable. With the right theory, the path would have light in the cloudiest of seasons. With the right level of collaboration and with our collective will and skill we could create a practice that is freedom within the belly of the beast. Perhaps then, with these in order "This is the Work" is not an opiate, but a spark to strategically light the flame of a slow burning coal.

Its use, for Bremner, is at once a celebration in good times, a reflection in confusing times and re-commitment in hard times. For example, in one tense exchange, toward the end of one these "seasons" in the year, Bremner was called out by a colleague in response to this mantra as essentially lack-luster and mediocre advice, especially from a leader.

Breathing deeply, he responded honestly that it was not an aspiration nor surrender, but for him it is a reckoning. For him, simply naming "the work" is both a reflection and an action, a stance and strategy, an analysis and a way forward through the gloom. For Bremner, it represents a key tension and balance between the patient and impatient—the need to address the Belly and the Beast simultaneously, which requires a belief and a relationship with the work to burn without burning out. It's a deep and ongoing reflection on his own identity, role and purpose along with a commitment to constructive collective struggle through leadership that taps our creativity, embraces an urgency tamed by the wisdom of practice, and is a reflection toward transformative action.

Being patient while impatient is paradox, a tension that needs to be held and it requires we do our work together. It is (re)committing to constructive work in the face of dysfunction to find a locus of impact. This dysfunction is not ahistorical, it is grounded deeply in the context of stolen lives, land, and a power structure, the DNA of this country that makes whiteness supremacy and its systems designed to maintain that power dynamic.

Author, educator, and whiteness interrogator, Robyn DiAngelo curates tangible lists that includes major decision-makers who are almost majority white and male in government, media, music, television, corporate ownership, wealthiest people, film makers, athletic team owners, and yes teachers and professors. As DiAngelo writes, "Race scholars use the term white supremacy to describe a sociopolitical economic system of domination based on racial categories that benefits those defined and perceived as white. This system of structural power privileges, centralizes, and elevates white people as a group" (Diangelo 2018, 30).

The education system plays a fundamental role in establishing and recreating racial hierarchies, status quo, and social categorization that expertly fails and blames the young people and communities it professes to uplift through a myth of meritocracy, biological essentialism, and performance in service of oppressive social constructions. Unless we address this and transform our role and the role of the education system from replicator to interrupter and transformer, that is preparing students for "college and career" that is white dominant, we are failing.

Radical social change has only come from the demands of Black, Indigenous, and People of Color (BIPOC), working people, women, and other groups that have had to resist in order to live, let alone thrive. Our work is to name, interrupt, and co-conspire with young people and in community to advance this work now and beyond.

THE WORK IS PERSONAL, BUT NOT PERSONALIZED

Bremner's high school experience was where race, culture, education, and his own reflective experience began to intersect and therefore develop his own racial consciousness. Growing up in a small, mostly white rural island town outside of Seattle, Washington, Bremner had limited exposure to BIPOC. Reflections on whiteness, his own or others, were minimal. For a variety of reasons, he ended up leaving that community and high school in his senior year to attend and graduate from a high school in South Seattle racially and economically diverse community.

Here he was both immersed in a diversity of cultures while at the same time beginning to recognize educational inequity and his privileges as a white person by what classes he was placed in and that he was a white person who could hoop. He loved playing basketball and he was decent, but Bremner didn't really push himself until he played in Seattle.

His basketball acumen, along with being a senior, allowed him to engage in different groups of friends and ultimately fit in quickly. He remembers thinking he wished he had made the move years earlier. Where he came from was not a bastion of high expectations and quality innovative teaching, but Bremner's experience at the Seattle school, along with his own developing consciousness about life and the world helped him to begin to see the world with a critical perspective.

One experience in particular was an English class where the students also received college credit. The teacher, a white woman, coming to the end of a fizzling career barely taught in class and allowed students to sleep with their heads down. Regardless, a paper was assigned and Bremner had a choice of topics, which at least allowed for the natural and critical thought of teenagers. Bremner decided to do in-person interviews around different religions and interviewed a teacher who was born again Christian and another who was a Buddhist.

In short, Bremner spent a lot of time on it, stayed up late, produced quality work and when he walked up to the teacher, she was sitting at a desk in the hallway. She took his paper, flipped through it and wrote "A" at the top. He was upset because his work was not validated or appreciated. For him, this highlights what he has come to understand as not only his own privilege but also the systems of education and inequity. It was a small action, but had lasting impacts on his understandings about background, education, experiences and the role, passion, and actions of a teacher.

That experience may be demonstrative of white male privilege or just the lazy low expectations of tired teacher or the inevitable low expectations within schools, cities, and systems of education. What is important is that it raises the questions for Bremner and continues to impact his thinking on how he approaches his purpose, his role, and his work.

Understanding himself, continuing to reflect, develop, grow, and learn through critical reflection, study and partnership with family, friends and peers is fundamental to how he survives and thrives and how he maintains sustainability and health. He attempts to question and be vulnerable as an ongoing lifelong learner with a deep appreciation for those doing the work that push him and grow him, especially as a cis-white man working with students of color in Oakland.

This then has developed and continues to develop his personal stance. He believes that in one light, privilege is poverty, and that burns deeply. A goal is to be "always waking" as Bremner's colleague and school leader Trevor Gardner describes in the book that accompanies this text. True wealth is shared intersectional experiences that celebrate the differences and commonalities of the human experience. He strives for co-liberation with others without romanticizing or glorifying. He believes education is the practice of freedom and this comes from disrupting systems of oppression, namely the hegemony that is white, capitalist, and a patriarchy.

He does this through his own self-love, joy, and seeking understanding of his place and that of others in our collective "co-liberation," to be his other self, and vice versa. To be a compassionate co-conspirator not an empathic ally. The personal is political for Bremner, deeply personal and therefore systemic. Bremner aims to challenge white supremacy through interrogation of his own thoughts and actions and in turn work with others through collective action to address systemic oppressions within education. DiAngelo writes:

> Rather than use what you see as unique about yourself as an exemption from further examination, a more fruitful approach would be to ask yourself, "I am white and I have X experience. How did X shape me as a result of also being white?" Setting aside your sense of uniqueness is a critical skill that will allow you to see the big picture of the society in which we live; individualism will not. For now, try to let go of your individual narrative and grapple with the collective messages we all receive as a member of a larger shared culture. Work to see how

these messages have shaped your life rather than use some aspect of your story to excuse yourself from their impact. (Diangelo 2018, 13)

This foundation supports his stance, approach, role, and ultimately work as an educator in the belly of the beast. As a white cis-gendered man Bremner is compliant and benefits in this system. It is his imperative to challenge and transform it. This has come from his weathering of the seasons, seeing cycles of design, redesign, and initiative fatigue while at the same time building, committing to best practice and pushing for a more engaging, relevant, and meaningful experience for youth within a system designed to fail. For Bremner then, his approach to doing the work starts with the following:

BOX 6.1 FOUNDATIONAL SUPPORTS

Personal Stance:

- The Beast exists and is active. Interrupt it in order to transform it.
- Be a co-conspirator in relation and partnership with youth, communities of color, and people most impacted by cis-gendered white male supremacy.
- Teaching and learning is lifelong. Make it constructive and with purpose.
- The political is personal, not personalized. It is systemic, so act collectively not individually.

Personal Approach:

- Reflect to act.
- Be humble and confident.
- Listen and affirm.
- Be critical and constructive.
- Interact with joy and humor.

Personal Roles:

- As a person: Communicate, study, live, have humor, and joy.
- As a teacher: Create a space that is engaging and has a purpose. Engage in participatory action research and design as a collective pedagogy, a process and a product rooted in students' lives and community.
- As a leader: Leverage resources, create structures, processes, and systems to align to a purpose through collaborative work based on shared beliefs and notions of success.

Bremner has weathered the seasons himself. At around the five-year wall mark as a teacher in Oakland, he began to realize that no matter how well he was doing in his class individually, it would not make any systematic changes, even within a small school environment. The siloing of teacher practice, curriculum, and student experience was burning him out, killing his inspiration and making education as an act of indoctrination not liberation. Knowing he was committed to education within the public school system, he looked for resources, networks, and supports to create community-based action research projects.

Ultimately, Bremner stumbled on the California Partnership Academy model supported by the State of California, now more widely known in Oakland as "Linked Learning Pathways." Academies and pathways were and have been a step closer to the collective and collaborative vision, stance, and action that both inspires Bremner's theory and grounds his practice.

Through a grant to the State of California, resources are allocated to create project-based learning, integrated projects, work-based learning, and career technical education. With these resources, structures and supports Bremner was able to write new courses, repurpose unused space on campus, purchase equipment, and support teachers and students through action toward a common mission and vision.

What became one of the two pathway programs at the school has a mission to: *Empower students through a highly rigorous, engaging and supportive learning environment to graduate prepared for college, career and life as designers and leaders of movements toward a sustainable and just world.* In addition, based on the success of this initial pathway, Bremner was tasked along with other teacher leaders to create a second pathway based in community health equity.

The pathways are now the two pillars of the school structure. Pathways are a structure to create collective and collaborative space based in teacher and ideally student leadership. They are a way to leverage resources, create a common language, open up collaborative meeting space, generate shared values and goals to provide a more engaging and meaningful experience for students.

This has become Bremner's work for over a decade and has kept him in the work, inspired and connected to groups of adults and students doing deeply important work around community design, housing, and gentrification, early childhood development, climate change, sustainability, land use, food systems and food access, social enterprise, action research, health equity, and relationships among many more. Education is the practice of freedom.

URGENCY IN THE LONG GAME—FOUNDATIONS
FOR HOLDING A PATIENT IMPATIENT TENSION

A key patient impatient tension is what Milton Reynolds, similarly as in chapter 1, has described as an "urgency in the long game." Oppressive systems are generations in the making and will be generations in the unmaking, while at the same time, and because of this historical reality, they also exist at crisis levels of urgency in life and death scenarios, literally. Education and the role of educators has been a core component of creating and replicating systems of oppression. The need to interrupt and transform the role and purpose of education is both immediate and long term. It must be day-to-day and it must also endure slow change.

As educators and education leaders we must hold this tension through the balance of theory and practice, long-term thinking and short-term actions. A balance that holds both the immediate and the generational aspects of "abolitionist work" guided by the "North Star" (Love 2019). Often in his career, Bremner has faced challenges to his reliance on theory as too vague, visionary, not getting work done, or too conceptual and time consuming. On the other hand, he has also faced challenges of moving too fast, being too detailed, and being too process- and/or product-oriented. Yet, theory is the guide. It is to what we connect our values, around which we build our collective stance, and on that we base our collaborative work.

For Bremner, critical theory is that which embraces the interplay of theory and practice to transform oppressive systems designed to categorize, marginalize, and silence into thriving systems that learn, support, and empower growth and fullest potential (hooks 1994). It is education as a practice of freedom in the service of participatory democracy (Dewey 1916; Freire 1970; Morrell 2008; Cammorata and Fine 2008).

With theory as a guide our stance must be one of an asset-based lifelong learner and constructive team member. It is partnering to develop and support autonomous learners. This stance tempers a wisdom through the slow burn of deep reflection, knowing self, time, commitment, and experience.

It's a perspective on the system and its impacts while staying in the work not only despite its failures, but because of its failures. It's a belief that this a coal, it's historic work and will not be solved in our lifetimes, while at the same time stoking the flame that is the project pilot, small win, and one at a time attempt and learning from the mistakes. How we show up every day— greetings with a smile at the door, asking questions and listening to youth, structured, engaging, and meaningful lesson plans wrapped in cariño through the warmth of high expectations—is where we as individuals literally and figuratively need to stand.

Similarly, the collective must stand. Common, vision, mission, and goals are key and even more so, common language, beliefs, and values founded and aligned in the collaborative effort, processes, and products that are collectively defined in order to build trust, create meaning, and serve youth and communities. The collective is co-conspiratorial, collectively accountable, and is willing to hold courageous conversations (Singleton 2005) based on relational trust and/or trust in collective process that works toward that relational trust.

The work is a deep reflection without analysis paralysis, clarity and questioning without distractions and tangents, structure and process without over agendizing and meeting fatigue. It is and/both not binary thinking that embraces multiple truths in the process of creative and constructive ideation and collective inspiration.

BALANCING THE TENSIONS: EMBRACE THE PARADOX OF "CONFLICTING TRUTHS" AND MULTIPLE PERSPECTIVES TO CO-CREATE

Intersectionality also allows educators to dialogue around a set of questions that will lead them to a better sense of their students' full selves, their students' challenges, the grace and beauty that is needed to juggle multiple identities seamlessly, and how schools perpetuate injustice. When teachers shy away from intersectionality, they shy away from ever fully knowing their students humanity and the richness of their students' identities. Mattering cannot happen if identities are isolated and students cannot be their full selves. (Love 2019, 7)

White supremacy plays out in many ways; however, in Bremner's work he is currently focusing on the theory and practice of collectivism and collaboration to create the best-learning experiences for adults and youth. In this light, the goal is collectivism that is decolonial, anti-racist, anti-white supremacist, empowering, and transformational for the people engaged in the work. One that is about embracing intersectionality through our practice together to create belonging and targeted universalism. Not color blind approaches to equity and inclusion but a commitment to and embracing of the tensions within the hegemony of white supremacy that we all must face given our place in the work.

A few of these tensions include individual versus collective, siloed versus collaborative, personal versus systemic, ahistorical versus historic, past versus present, and competition versus community. These are false dichotomies but tensions all the same as they are complicated, ingrained in our various identities, mind states, and actions. Given the complexity of experience, story, interpretation, and multiple perspectives there are inherently many truths to both embrace and to disrupt. Bremner believes that through a collaborative process of meaning making, shared experience, and practice a collective truth that best serves youth and communities will emerge.

THE WORK IS COLLECTIVE: NOBODY'S COMING; IT'S JUST US

Bremner calls for a critically collective and collaborative effort as a means to do anti-white supremacist intersectionally liberatory work. It is to be within the beast in order to transform it; to embrace and explore the tensions that are multiple experiences, identities, perspectives, and personalities based on a collective will, common word, and collaborative action.

For Bremner, the word *collective* is an understanding, stance, value, and belief, while the word *collaboration* is a form of being and acting based on service of a collective belief and value system.

This is what ultimately challenges and aims to transform the oppression of intersectionality and hetero white male capitalist hegemonic norms and structures. Much has been written on Professional Learning Communities, Communities of Practice, Small Learning Communities among others. At the core, Bremner believes that community serves the collective in the most basic ways. As educational and systems leader Fred Brill writes:

> Professional learning communities can meet so many basic human needs" the need for a sense of belonging and acceptance, the need for esteem based on the learning and growth, the need to serve a higher moral purpose, and the need for meaning in our work and our lives. If his sounds vaguely familiar, it is because it calls to mind Maslow (1943) and his hierarchy of needs." The levels that include basic needs, then safety, love and acceptance and finally self-actualization. (Brill 2008, 14)

Defining how we collaborate and how we act is core to the work and grounds our collective liberation. What makes effective teams in any given context takes common language, shared learning, and meaning making as we create the path. We need each other to address and expose our individual needs and challenges in parallel to addressing those of the Beast. For example, Jones and Okun (2001) outline what many would recognize as a "professional" work environment as aspects of white supremacist cultural norms, including a "sense of urgency, defensiveness, either/or thinking, fear of open conflict and individualism" among others.

This urgency is individual, replicates status quo, and are quick fix technical solutions that mimic change but do little to truly change dynamics of access and power. This is different than a collective sense of urgency, as described earlier, that is based on an anti-racist analysis and immediacy driven by centuries of oppressions. These oppressions evolve and are masked by "professionalism" and are only flushed out and directly addressed through multiple perspectives and collective work. If Collectivism is value, then Collaboration is an action that is fundamental in creating process, structures, environments, and experiences to best serve youth and community.

Coming from an alternative education system that served young people officially failed by district systems, the small schools movement lured Bremner into teaching within the Oakland Unified School District's iteration of the Beast. Seeing an opportunity that was small, manageable, and potentially transformative, the small schools established collective spaces for youth and adults to work together toward common goals. A vast majority of those schools are now closed.

A critique of that movement, successes and challenges will be saved for a different book, but a lesson learned for Bremner was both how the small school innovation both served the Beast and also provided some light to lead the way. On the one hand, that small school merely attempted to replicate what larger dysfunctional schools do, just smaller. On the other, it did provide a unique experience of community and home for adults and youth alike. In addition to anecdotal evidence from a former student, who is now a colleague, Bremner reflects on one experience that continues to shed some light on his practice.

In the last semester of the final year of the school that was closed in what became the crashing implosion of the small schools' movement in Oakland, Bremner led the design, facilitated and participated in an interdisciplinary project-based learning pilot based in the lived conditions of students and the history of Oakland.

In short, the level of collaboration around collectively defined goals, both held an expectation for teachers and instruction at the same time holding an expectation of excellence for student work, all in the midst of school closure. For Bremner, it was one of the most successful teaching and collaborating experiences of student presentation and authentic demonstration of learning. Despite it, literally, being the last class of the last project of the last day of that school, teachers and students showed up.

Students and teachers together were able to present, discuss, reflect, and celebrate a critically relevant project that brought all the disciplines together to research, analyze, and recommend solutions that impacted Oakland. Equally important was when they didn't show up. They saw it and knew it themselves at a level of self-reflection and internal collective accountability as demanded by a project that is collaboratively defined, implemented, and demonstrated.

For example, one teacher through demonstration of student work as part of the integrated project, realized and reflected how they had not followed through on the agreements and had therefore effectively dropped the ball. If only the team had the chance to iterate and do it again! The Beast consumed that possibility. Oakland Unified is experiencing the impact of that implosion, confusion, and now attempt to redesign yet again a learning experience for its youth, families, and community.

If nobody is coming and it's just us—how do we support others to embrace this? Lean into leadership? Do this as a group with others? These are questions Bremner tackles daily working with pathway leadership teams and pathway teams. To go alone is to replicate a system of injustice and disconnection. School reforms and initiatives will come and go, there must be a throughline. For Bremner this throughline is creating structures for collective work to engage young people in authentic and meaningful action.

His goal is not to create pathway programs alone, but to create systems, structures, and processes to implement a collective will in service of young people and communities. For him, for now; those are called pathways. Ultimately it is about creating a school of education and learning, not a school for more school. From the Art of Coaching Teams by Elena Aguilar a long time Oakland educator:

> When I think back on the places where change was made and children got more of what they need and deserve, those were uniformly places where the adults at the site worked in high-functioning teams together and where there was a respect and trust between teachers and between teachers and administrators. In those places, when storms hit (and they did), the communities of adults and children weathered them well and emerged stronger than before . . . . At those moments, from within those healthy communities, I observed firsthand the positive impact of good teams on our children. (Aguilar 2016, XXV)

RECKONING WITH THE BEAST: CRITICAL COLLABORATION THROUGH CRITICAL PRAXIS

Asa Hilliard, professor of educational psychology and African History, writes in his reflective questioning about a collective will to educate all children. He describes "deep restructuring" and the attitudes, beliefs, and ultimately collaboration in order to serve young people. Furthermore, he asserts that "teachers need their own intellectual and emotional hunger fed. They need to experience the joy of collaborative discussion, dialogue, critique and research." In this context, this merging of the idea with the practice, words with actions, process and product is the reckoning. The deep level of belief and value work to contradict, interrupt, transform notions of power, privilege, and ultimately white supremacy.

> The restructuring that educators need to do, then, is much more a matter of theory, philosophy, perception, conception, assumptions, and models than it is a matter of rearranging the technical and logistical chairs on the educational Titanic. It is not a matter of the amount of time, of middle schools or junior high schools, of site-based management of schools of choice, of behavioral objectives, or access to technology. Deep restructuring is a matter of drawing up an appropriate vision of human potential, of designing human institutions of creating a professional work environment, of the linking of school activities with communities directions, of creating human bonds in the operation of appropriate socialization activities and of aiming for the stars for the children and for ourselves academically and socially. (Hillard 1995, 203)

School site leadership comes in many forms and is paramount in developing and sustaining quality schools. School sites are unique ecosystems encompassing myriad complex systems within a very special localized context. Disregarding these unique strengths and challenges is one of the key missteps of district and systems leaders in attempts to scale, measure, and quantify learning relationships and environments: to perform. The work can easily become overly technical responses to external expectations, needs and pressures and not the deeper transformational work needed to base school in relevant, sustaining education that holistically serves young people and community.

School leadership is key in holding this space, expectation, boundary, and sanctuary for learning, of youth and adults alike. This work is based on beliefs, values, and purpose of the people and the place. Granted this leadership work is profoundly connected the technical and operational needs of a school. This work is collective and must be done in partnership. Perhaps more importantly, then it's the questions that we ask ourselves, our staff, students, and communities that is most important. Why are we here, what and how are we going to do this together?

PARTNERSHIP WITH YOUTH: ACTION RESEARCH AND DESIGN THINKING

Critical Praxis (Friere 1970) is a professional throughline for Bremner since he first began in youth development work over two decades ago. As a vision and an action Bremner has used participatory action research and design as a way to frame the work, organize and engage communities, enliven classrooms and create space for agency that has transformed his practice and some of the spaces where he has had the privilege to work and therefore learn.

Through processes of defining research methodologies with youth who are most impacted by the research creates a dynamic learning space together in partnership around issues most relevant to the community with a goal of developing autonomous learners reaching their highest potential. And, to be transparent, working in partnership with youth to support and develop them as co-conspirators now and beyond. Used as professional approach, classroom pedagogy and leadership strategy, action research and design through collective and collaborative processes has yielded the most inspiring projects, products, and processes in Bremner's career. This too is *the work*.

One example includes an acre produce farm at the East Oakland school that was initially conceived, designed, and created by the students and community partners in the pathway program founded by Bremner, which was itself inspired by student voice and call—formally (feedback, interviews, surveys, discussions) and informally (not showing up to school, low grades and growth, disengagement in classes in general).

Another example is a project started in Bremner's Government/Economics class that has now become the Senior Seminar Project at East Oakland High School where students create a year-long project based on action research design, methodology, and action (through an internship) to address the issues most important to their lives. In these examples students read the "world and the word" (Freire 1987) and their lives along with secondary and primary source research documentation and data collection become the text and the curriculum for the course.

Lastly, as part of the Career Technical Education classes Bremner developed as the core of the pathway experience, he used Tupac's Rose and Concrete as a metaphor students complete quantitative and qualitative research around, in one case, air quality, in order to set the foundation for designing hedgerows on the farm that will create natural beautiful boundaries, patches for carbon sequestration and areas for local pollinators like bees and butterflies to support the growth of a sustainable food system on campus.

Meanwhile, laser cut and 3D printed models of roses and concrete were designed and manufactured to physically portray the idea, research findings were written up in essays, and collaborative group work on the paper. Digging in the soil and planting in the earth as hands-on application to connect with nature and build sustainably was completed to grow our skills and knowledge in the process of growing our school, community, and world. The world is the word and this is the work.

PARTNERSHIP WITH ADULTS: BUILDING SMALL LEARNING COMMUNITIES AND PATHWAYS

Currently in Oakland, the most recent design initiative is "Linked Learning" or College and Career Pathways buttressed by the passing of a Measure N, a city property tax ballot initiative approved by Oakland voters to fund pathway programs at high schools based on the four pillars of "Rigorous Academics, Comprehensive Student Supports, Work Based Learning and Career Technical Education." Unlike the small schools movement that established schools as separate entities each with their own operational structures, the pathway initiative builds pathways or small learning communities within schools based on common themes. For the past four years, Bremner has worked as Pathway Coach at East Oakland High School.

A motivating factor for taking the job was that it was primarily site based, but also allowed for the time necessary to build out quality programs without teaching full time as he had been doing for the previous twelve years. In addition, in working with the other coaches representing the other major high schools in Oakland, the work also allowed for very informed systems level experience and analysis, given we were all deeply involved with the design and implementation of our specific school initiatives and also our collective minds and experiences most accurately captured what was happening district wide.

From this came adjusting and adapting best practice systems analysis frames such as the 6th Circle Model (Wheatley 1999) to name both transactional and transformational leadership actions with additional all-encompassing 7th Circle to represent the underlining social-economic conditions of the lived experiences of the youth we aimed to serve.

With a transformative systems analysis came the identification of a series of specific conditions for leadership, such as clear systems of evaluation, communication, and accountability to the community, in order to fully realize the vision of pathway programs that prepare young people for "college, career and community."

Having founded and been deeply involved in the development of the pathway programs at the school, Bremner's work now is to further design and implement these programs. Bremner maintains the importance of community through collaboration that drew him to small schools in the first place and continues to drive his work now. In this light, pathways are primarily setting up structures that are one step closer to collaborative work.

Pathways are not the point, the resources, structures, and expectations to collaborate around common themes, processes, and outcomes for students is the point. Getting adults to buy in and engage in collective work has been a formidable challenge. Time, identities, personalities, experience, attitudes, skills, and values among others all play a complicated role in challenging collective collaboration.

Relying on listening stance and pushing constructive attitudes and dialogue Bremner works with teams of teachers and teacher leaders to hold a space that is both flexible and structured, that uses common processes but remains authentic, that is both linear and cyclical in order to differentiate, engage, and meet adults within their own Zones of Proximal Development in the profession of teaching and the work of collective action.

Grubb and Tredway describe the history, context and lived experience of a collective and collaborative school as one that comes from historic and collective movements for justice "committed to the exercise of political and social power through collaboration" where "individuals have conversations about race, identity, and privilege and are committed to work together towards justice" (Grubb and Tredway 2010). This work includes both internal and external issues and dynamics ranging from different personalities and perspectives to an understanding of school reform and public policy.

These are the schools that create systems for Freedom Dreaming that both offer and create inclusive counternarratives that address the lived experiences of students and communities. These are schools that are at once the Beast and Battle the Beast. These schools have common ground, actions, and tools to work from a collective stance in collaborative transformative action in the service of social justice.

CONCLUSION

In a simple metaphorical sense, the Beast is a manifestation of what grows it, nourishes it, sustains it—the Belly. To battle the Beast we must primarily know and attack the Belly using the collective conceptions, frames, theories, practices, and tools while also pushing to transform the Beast into whatever vision we co-construct. This requires a balanced dosage to remedy the beast. *The Work*, according to Bremner, is the balance of many tensions that require both patience and impatience.

Embracing these tensions through embracing personal reflection and collective theory and practice is proven best practice, anti-racist, collaborative, and intersectional. It is concocting the remedy from within. It is leaning into one another as colleagues, co-conspirators, and organic intellectuals to "make the road while walking" (Horton and Freire 1990) in our shared practice, learning, and growing. In that spirit is at once the culmination of twenty years of work in the profession and a snapshot of where Bremner is today. What he has read and what he is reading, what he knows, what he is learning, and what he has yet to figure out.

REFLECTIVE QUESTIONS FOR LEADING
IN THE BELLY OF THE BEAST

1. How do you reflect on your own theories and practices? How do these both support and challenge your identity, values, and beliefs? Where do you need to be more patient and/or more impatient?
2. What is your personal stance as an educator? How is this lived with youth and adults on site? What authors and theories guide your practice? In turn, what are key pedagogies or strategies that make up your practice?
3. Is there a collective stance or vision at your site? How is your personal stance aligned (or not) to a collective stance (explicit or implicit) on campus?
4. Who are colleagues who practice a collectivism and act collaboratively? Where are collaborative spaces/bodies on campus? Where are opportunities to transform or create these spaces on campus? How are you in partnership with youth and BIPOC?
5. How does this Beast manifest in yourself, in your practice and at your site? What are you doing daily to battle and transform this? Who are the co-conspirators in your personal and professional life to help you?

References

Leading in the Belly of the Beast

INTRODUCTION

Baldwin, James. *Baldwin – Collected Essays/Notes of A Native Son/Nobody Knows My Name/The Fire Next Time/No Name in the Street/The Devil Finds Work.* The Library of America, New York, NY, 1998.

Jefferson, Thomas. *Notes On Virginia.* viii, 388. Ford Ed., iii, 251 (1782), as quoted in *The Jefferson Cyclopedia, a Comprehensive Collection of the Views of Thomas Jefferson,* edited by John P. Foley. Funk and Wagnalls Company, New York, 1900.

CHAPTER 1—THE DANGERS OF DEFINITION

Chapman, Paul Davis. 1988. *Schools As Sorters: Lewis M. Terman, Applied Psychology, and the Intelligence Testing Movement, 1890–1930.* New York University Press.

Eberhardt, Jennifer. 2005. "Imaging Race." *American Psychologist* 60(2) (February–March 2005): 182.

Fay, Laura. 2018. "What's the Racial Breakdown of America's Public School Teachers?" *T74,* August 14, 2018. https://www.the74million.org/article/whats-the-racial-breakdown-of-americas-public-school-teachers/.

Gordon, Leah N. 2019. "Causality, Context, and Colorblindness." In *Seeing Race Again: Countering Colorblindness across the Disciplines,* edited by Kimberle Williams Crenshaw, Luke Charles Harris, Daniel Martinez HoSang, and George Lipsitz, 227–31. Oakland: University of California Press.

Haller, Mark. 1965. *Eugenics: Hereditarian Attitudes in American Thought.* Rutgers University Press.

Kamin, Leon. 1974. *The Science and Politics of I.Q.* Lawrence Erlbaum Associates, Inc.

Lipsitz, George. 2019. "The Sound of Silence: How Race Neutrality Preserves White Supremacy." In *Seeing Race Again: Countering Colorblindness across the Disciplines*, edited by Kimberlé Williams Crenshaw, Luke Charles Harris, Daniel Martinez HoSang, and George Lipsitz, 40–41. Oakland: University of California Press.

Loewen, James. 2018. *Teaching What Really Happened: How to Avoid the Tyranny of Textbooks and Get Students Excited About Doing History*. New York: Teachers College Press, 10–17.

Loewen, James, and Sebesta, Edward H. 2011. *The Confederate and Neo-Confederate Reader: The Great "Truth" and the "Lost Cause."* University Press Mississippi, 20.

Reynolds, Milton. 2019. "Shifting Frames: Pedagogical Interventions in Colorblind Teaching Practice." In *Seeing Race Again: Countering Colorblindness across the Disciplines*, edited by Kimberlé Williams Crenshaw, Luke Charles Harris, Daniel Martinez HoSang, and George Lipsitz, 354–59. Oakland: University of California Press.

Selden, Steven. 1999. *Inheriting Shame: The Story of Eugenics in America*. New York: Teachers College Press.

Sensoy, Ozlem, and DiAngelo, Robin. 2014. "Respecting Differences?: Challenging the Common Guidelines in Social Justice Education." *Democracy and Education* 22(2): 1–10. https://democracyeducationjournal.org/home/vol22/iss2/1.

Steele, Claude M. 2010. *Whistling Vivaldi And Other Cues to How Stereotypes Affect Us*. W.W. Norton & Company, Inc.

Stoskopf, Alan. 2002. *Race and Membership in American History: The Eugenics Movement*. Facing History And Ourselves National Foundation, Inc.

Terman, Lewis M. 1916. *The Measurement of Intelligence*. Boston: Houghton Mifflin.

CHAPTER 2—FOCUS ON THE CORE: LEADING TOWARD COMMUNITY, SOLIDARITY, AND PURPOSE

Bowles, Samuel, and Herbert Gintiss. 2012. *Schooling in Capitalist America: Educational Reforms and the Contradictions of Economic Life*. Chicago: Haymarket Books.

Eubanks, Eugene, Ralph Parrish, and Diane Smith. 1997. *Race, Ethnicity, and Multiculturalism: Policy and Practice*, edited by Peter Hall. Missouri Symposium on Research and Educational Policy, Routledge.

Hammond, Zaretta, and Yvette Jackson. 2015. *Culturally Responsive Teaching and the Brain: Promoting Authentic Engagement and Rigor among Culturally and Linguistically Diverse Students*. Thousand Oaks, CA: Corwin.

Noguera, Pedro A. (Guest Editor). 2017. Introduction to "Racial Inequality and Education: Patterns and Prospects for the Future." *The Educational Forum* 81(2): 129–35.

Safir, Shane. 2017. *Listening Leader Creating the Conditions for Equitable School Transformation*. San Francisco: John Wiley & Sons.

Wheatley, M., and T. Dalmau. 1983. *The Six-Circle Model*. Dalmau Consulting. https://www.dalmau.com/six-circle-model/

Wheatley, Margaret. 2001. "Restoring Hope to the Future Through Critical Education of Leaders." https://www.margaretwheatley.com/articles/restoringhope.html.

CHAPTER 3—LEADING WITH "TENACIOUS LOVE"

Blankstein, Alan M., et al. 2016. *Excellence through Equity: Five Principles of Courageous Leadership to Guide Achievement for Every Student*. ASCD.

Cisneros, Sandra. 1989. *The House on Mango Street*. New York: Vintage Books.

Cleland, Max. *Strong at the Broken Places*. Longstreet Press, 2000.

Hammond, Zaretta, and Yvette Jackson. 2015. *Culturally Responsive Teaching and the Brain: Promoting Authentic Engagement and Rigor among Culturally and Linguistically Diverse Students*. Corwin, a SAGE Company.

Monroe, Dr. Lorraine. 1997. *Nothing's Impossible: Leadership Lessons from Inside and Outside the Classroom*. Public Affairs, a member of the Perseus Book Group.

CHAPTER 4—THE FREEDOM TO THINK CRITICALLY

Barr, Dennis, Boulay, Beth, Selman, Robert, McCormick, Rachel, Lowenstein, Ethan, Gamse, Beth, Fine, Melinda, and Leonard, M. Brielle. 2015. "A Randomized Controlled Trial of Professional Development for Interdisciplinary Civic Education: Impacts on Humanities Teachers and Their Students." *Teachers College Record*, v117, n2.

Ferlazzo, Larry. 2015. "Response: Teachers Stay Because 'They Made a Choice to Serve.'" *Education Week Teacher*. May 16, 2015. http://blogs.edweek.org/teachers/classroom_qa_with_larry_ferlazzo/2015/05/response_teachers_stay_because_they_made_a_choice_to_serve.html.

Leska, Samantha. Interview. May 23, 2019.

McFeely, Shane. 2018. "Why Your Best Teachers Are Leaving and 4 Ways to Keep Them." *Gallup*. March 27, 2018. https://www.gallup.com/education/237275/why-best-teachers-leaving-ways-keep.aspx.

Smagorinsky, Peter. 2017. "Get Schooled" Column. *AJC*. https://www.ajc.com/blog/get-schooled/defeated-too-many-students-and-scripted-instruction-good-teacher-becomes-teacher/gKZrT406yvwzKLvoM7xLEI/.

Strauss, Valerie. 2013. "Teacher Slams Scripted Common Core Lessons that Must be Taught 'Word for Word'." *Washington Post*. November 30, 2013. https://www.washingtonpost.com/news/answer-sheet/wp/2013/11/30/teacher-slams-scripted-common-core-lessons-that-must-be-taught-word-for-word/.

Strauss, Valerie. 2015. "Why So Many Teachers Leave – and How to Get Them to Stay." *Washington Post*. June 12, 2015. https://www.washingtonpost.com/news/answer-sheet/wp/2015/06/12/why-so-many-teachers-leave-and-how-to-get-them-to-stay/?noredirect=on.

CHAPTER 5—STUDENTS IN THE CENTER

Crenshaw, Kimberlé. "Kimberlé Crenshaw on Intersectionality Over Two Decades Later." Interview with African American Policy Forum. Colombia Law School, June 8, 2017. https://www.law.columbia.edu/pt-br/news/2017/06/kimberle-crenshaw-intersectionality.

Crenshaw, Kimberlé. "The Urgency of Intersectionality." Filmed October 2016 at TEDWomen 2016. Video, 18:41. https://www.ted.com/talks/kimberle_crenshaw_the_urgency_of_intersectionality?language=ry.

DiAngelo, Robin. "White Fragility." *The International Journal of Critical Pedagogy* 3, no. 3 (2011): 54–70.

Feldman, Joe. 2019. *Grading for Equity: What It Is, Why It Matters, and How It Can Transform Schools and Classrooms.* Thousand Oaks, CA: Corwin.

Guo, Winona, and Vulchi, Priya. 2019. *Tell Me Who You Are: Sharing Our Stories of Race, Culture, and Identity.* New York: Penguin.

Hammond, Zaretta. 2014. *Culturally Responsive Teaching and the Brain: Promoting Authentic Engagement and Rigor among Culturally and Linguistically Diverse Students.* Thousand Oaks, CA: Corwin.

Knight, Jim. 2011. *Unmistakable Impact: A Partnership Approach for Dramatically Improving Instruction.* Thousand Oaks, CA: Corwin.

Love, Bettina L. 2019. *We Want to Do More Than Survive: Abolitionist Teaching and the Pursuit of Educational Freedom.* Boston, MA: Beacon Press.

Robbins, Pam and Alvy, Harvey B. 2014. *The Principal's Companion: Strategies to Lead Schools for Student and Teacher Success.* Thousand Oaks, CA: Corwin.

Tatem, Beverly Daniel. 1997. *Why Are All the Black Kids Sitting Together in the Cafeteria: And Other Conversations About Race.* New York: Basic Books.

Tervalon, Melanie, and Murray-Garcia, Jann. "Cultural Humility Versus Cultural Competence: A Critical Distinction in Defining Physician Training Outcomes in Multicultural Education." *Journal of Health Care for the Poor and Underserved* 9, no. 2 (May 1998): 117–25.

CHAPTER 6—"THIS IS THE WORK": A PERSONAL AND PROFESSIONAL WORKING FOR SUSTAINING IN THE BELLY OF THE BEAST

Aguilar, Elena. 2016. *The Art of Coaching Teams: Building Resilient Communities that Transform Schools.* San Francisco: Jossey-Bass.

Brill, Fred. 2008. *Leading and Learning: Effective School Leadership Through Reflective Storytelling and Inquiry.* Stenhouse Publishers.

Cammarota, Julio, and Michelle Fine. 2008. *Revolutionizing Education: Youth Participatory Action Research in Action.* New York: Routledge.

Dewey, John. 1916. *Democracy and Education: An Introduction to the Philosophy of Education.* Macmillan.

DiAngelo, Robin. 2018. *White Fragility: Why It's So Hard for White People to Talk About Racism*. Boston: Beacon Press.

Freire, Paulo. 1970. *Pedagogy of the Oppressed*. New York: Continuum.

Freire, Paulo, and Donaldo Macedo. 1987. *Literacy: Reading the Word and the World*. Westport: Bergin and Garvey.

Grubb, W. Norton, and Lynda Tredway. 2010. *Leading from the Inside Out: Expanded Roles for Teachers in Equitable Schools*. New York: Routledge.

Hilliard, Asa. 1995. *The Maroon Within Us: Selected Essays on African American Community Socialization*. Black Classic Press.

Hooks, Bell. 1994. *Teaching to Transgress: Education as the Practice of Freedom*. New York: Routledge.

Horton, Myles, and Paulo Freire. 1990. *We Make the Road by Walking: Conversations on Education and Social Change*. Temple University Press.

Love, Bettina. 2019. *We Want to Do More Than Survive: Abolitionist Teaching and the Pursuit of Educational Freedom*. Boston: Beacon Press.

Morrell, Ernest. 2008. *Critical Literacy and Urban Youth: Pedagogies of Access, Dissent, and Liberation*. New York: Routledge.

Singleton, Glen. 2005. *Courageous Conversations about Race: A Field Guide for Achieving Equity in Schools*. Thousand Oaks: Corwin.

Wheatley, Margaret. 1999. *Leadership and the New Science: Discovering Order in a Chaotic World*. San Francisco: Berrett-Koehler Publishers.

About the Contributors

Eran DeSilva comes from an immigrant family who came to the United States from Sri Lanka when she was a year old. She is bicultural—very much immersed in American culture but with core cultural values from her Sinhalese roots. She has biracial children—a fact that has continued to shape her identity as she helps them bridge the diversity within her own nuclear and extended family. Being from Sri Lanka makes her a minority among minorities. Because of this, she has learned to build bridges and community among diverse people in order to create a sense of belonging.

DeSilva has a masters in teaching from University of San Francisco and has been in the field of education for eighteen years. She currently is the director of Professional Development and a social studies teacher at Notre Dame High School, San Jose.

Kristin Botello is a third-generation Chicana, who was born, raised, and continues to live in East Los Angeles. She grew up in a Mexican American, Catholic home, the youngest of nine children. She is a member of a huge extended family consisting of mostly educators and artists. She has been married for twenty-seven years.

She is a parent to three amazing children, who continue to give her purpose and who have joined her in her mission of nurturing creative expression and growing young minds in service of community. One of the greatest learning experiences in her life has been as the mother of a son with autism. Her son has taught her unending patience, faith, persistence; he has taught her what it means to learn from and approach the world differently, which only strengthens her work as an educator.

Botello brings thirty years of teaching experience to her chapter. She is currently the principal of Animo Jackie Robinson Charter High School and has served as a school leader in Los Angeles for the last thirteen years.

Meredith Gavrin grew up as a white, Jewish girl from the suburbs of New York and became a somewhat ineffective teacher in her first year in a New York City public school after attending graduate school. For the love of her students and her fervent belief that every student deserves equal access to a high-quality, potentially life-changing, public education, she kept working at it, and gradually became a better teacher and then a school co-founder and leader.

She is now the proud mother of three biracial, interfaith children: Elijah, Caleb, and Mia. She is a twenty-year resident of the City of New Haven, Connecticut, and a proud co-founder, along with her husband, Greg Baldwin, of New Haven Academy, a public, interdistrict magnet high school. The school was one of the first members of Facing History's Innovative Schools Network (now Partner Schools Network), and Gavrin has served on the advisory board of the network for the last several years. She received her bachelor's degree at Princeton University and her MEd at Harvard University and has worked in education for more than twenty-five years.

Milton Reynolds is a polymathic, San Francisco Bay Area, born and based, cis-gendered, married, African American educator and community servant. As one who loves the complexity of difficult problems, and the exhilaration of learning, he found school to be an uninviting and unwelcoming place. Since ideas are free, he sought them elsewhere and continues to do so, linking up along the way with other visionary educators who share a passion for justice, equity, and the belief that we can create whatever sort of community we desire.

His lifelong investment in the development of young people and community engagement is fueled by an unending belief in the power of the collective agency and imagination. Reynolds is a career educator, counselor, and curriculum design specialist with over twenty-five years of classroom experience. He has led reform initiatives in the areas of education, community development and response, and law enforcement.

Timothy Bremner is from the Pacific Northwest and has become an adult in Oakland, CA, for the past twenty years. As a white heterosexual cis-gendered man, he works for a present and a future, where one's life outcomes are not predetermined by skin color or other social constructions. Teaching and education has become the way that he can channel the urgency he feels into social systems change and to make his daily personal and professional life align with his values of justice, freedom, and sustainability.

Bremner shares his life with his spouse and two children. He has been working in the Oakland Unified School District as teacher, academy director, and pathway coach since 2003. Having founded the Sustainable Urban Design Academy (SUDA) at Castlemont High School in East Oakland, he is now a Linked Learning Pathway Coach responsible for working with students, teacher teams, and leadership teams to continue the development of SUDA and supporting the development of a second pathway on campus, the Community Health Equity Academy (CHEA).

Trevor Gardner has always believed that education is the most powerful way to transform society to be more just, healthy, and equitable. This is why he chose to become a teacher and why he has committed his life to teaching and leading in schools in the Bay Area for over twenty years.

Gardner is a white, heterosexual, cis-gendered man who grew up in a small town in Northern California. In this society, that means he has immense unearned privilege. He continually wrestles with how to manifest the responsibility that comes with this privilege in ways that are honest, humble, and genuinely impactful.

Gardner has called Oakland home for the past fifteen years. He has been in a biracial relationship with his life partner and mother of his twelve-year-old son since 2002—a family dynamic that continually transforms and redefines how he understands identity. He has come to see identity as an evolution, a continual process of becoming, through critical self-reflection on the relationship between self, others, and the world around him.

Gardner taught high school English and history starting in 1999 and transitioned into school leadership after fifteen years in the classroom. He is currently the director of Teaching and Learning at ARISE High School in East Oakland. He is the author of *Discipline over Punishment: Successes and Struggles with Restorative Justice in Schools*, published in 2017 by Rowman and Littlefield.